ENJ

EVERYTHING

Biblical Lessons on Giving

JANET M. MAGIERA

LWM Publications
Irvine, California

LWM Publications is a division of
Light of the Word Ministry
4152 Manzanita St.
Irvine CA 92604
(949) 510-5693

Cover Photo by Angel Penatch

Library of Congress No : 00-92019

ISBN No. 0-9679613-0-0

Printed in the United States by
Morris Publishing
3212 East Highway 30
Kearney, NE 68847
1-800-650-7888

And God is able to make all grace abound toward you; that ye, always having all sufficiency in all things, may abound to every good work:…Being enriched in every thing to all bountifulness, which causeth through us thanksgiving to God.
-----II Corinthians 9:8, 11

Forward

The first question most readers would ask themselves in reading the title of this book, "Enriched in Everything, " might be, "Is my life enriched in everything? " Knowing that this is God's will for His people, if there are areas in our lives that seem less than enriched, the last place we might want to consider as root causes upon which we need more light may be lessons on giving. Some have defined a rich man as "one who has no need." One can be very wealthy and still have areas of life that are empty, unfulfilled, and hopeless.

The title of this book, *Enriched in Everything,* is the end result of the application of all of the principles discussed in the lessons on giving. It comes from II Corinthians 9:8-10. The verse that is quoted the most is "grace should abound." Why did we not read the rest of the context? When God pours out his grace for every good work, then the person has something to give – both seed and bread. The completeness of the supply is poured out! Then BEING enriched, it causes great thankfulness to God. This is the way we can see how to help people in this area.

If there is great thankfulness abounding in a person's life, they are practicing these principles. If not, we can backtrack to determine the problem. It starts with being motivated by love and then to practice GIVING. Many types of giving are discussed in the book: giving to get, giving from fear, giving because of pressure from others. The only giving that works is that which is in obedience to our Father and Lord Jesus Christ and is done with faith. This is the first lesson and it goes on from there.

The reader will find thought-provoking and heart-searching questions at the end of each chapter that will challenge personal growth and commitment. Each chapter is a valuable resource for study groups that will inspire further study and discussion, providing stepping stones for all of us towards a II Corinthians 9:8 lifestyle, enriched in everything.

Sheryl Singleton
Las Vegas, Nevada
May 2000

Table of Contents

Introduction

Setting the Premise

Passages to Study: John 3:16-21

When I was a new Christian, I had been going through some tough times financially and had several large bills that were due by a certain date. If these were not paid, I would not be able to continue in my schooling at the time. I remember asking an acquaintance of mine, who never seemed to have any troubles with money, "Why is it that you are never worried about finances?" He then shared with me that his father was fairly wealthy and had always provided everything that he had ever needed all his life. There never was a time when he was not confident that his parents would be able to take care of his needs. He had transferred this confidence and trust to God now that he was an adult. He said that he just presented the needs to God and then believed that God would take care of them and show him what to do if needed. It dawned on me that even though I was giving lip service to the idea that God was able to meet my needs, I did not have this confidence.

I never have forgotten this incident because it was a turning point in my life. At that time, I learned to apply the verse, **"you have not, because you ask not" (James 4:2).** What had shaken me about this incident was that I realized I did not really believe that God as my Father was now my provider in every category. No matter <u>what</u> I needed, He would provide! Throughout the years, I have endeavored to build that confidence from study in the Bible about the different aspects of giving. There were several periods of time when I studied this subject consistently, because of great need in my life.

This book is the result of another one of these study periods, not because we had such great need, but because I desired to be able to teach these principles to others, who had questions and needed answers. Many of the lessons in this book have added to my own understanding also and have challenged me to ask for wisdom in how to apply them.

That is the purpose for the book: to challenge you as the reader to think about the lessons and to cry out for wisdom on how to apply them FOR YOU. I have chosen not to write many personal incidents or to describe situations that I have known about personally, because in this study, my prayer is that God will bring your own incidents and situations to mind, and these will be more pertinent that any I could share.

These lessons are to be used for personal or group study. The format is very simple. First there are passages to read. Then the lesson can be studied and pondered. Lastly, there are study questions, which are designed to generate thoughtfulness, prayer, and discussion. I have also endeavored not to highlight my own beliefs and conclusions exclusively. My heart is to have the Word do the teaching and confronting, if necessary. I expect that whether you believe in tithing or not, whether you give to a Church or minister or not, these lessons will apply to you. It is not my intention to tear apart your current beliefs, but please just consider the lesson and allow God to show you how it relates to you personally.

There are thirteen lessons in the book. I had wanted to divide the number of chapters evenly between Old and New Testaments, but this is not how it ended up. There are seven chapters from the Old Testament and the seventh is regarding all of the bountiful blessings that result from giving. There are six chapters from the New Testament. The first of these is actually a combination of two passages from both Old and New Testament and represents a "new beginning" as chapter 8. So there are really 7 + 1 + 5 lessons. They build in sequence and each lesson relates to the previous ones. It is not that you could not study them out of order, but to see the whole picture, it is best to go through them systematically.

SETTING THE PREMISE

Giving

The verb "to give" paints a very beautiful, simple picture. If you hold out your hand with something in it, and you place it in someone else's hand, that is giving. First of all, you must have something in your hand. Then, the "something" must leave your hand; otherwise it is not giving. What the other person does with the gift is not part of the process. This picture applies to many categories of things that are not strictly physical. Teaching is giving, comfort is giving, and love is giving. The basic picture applies in every case, however. The best way to begin these lessons is to consider the example of God, our Father.

John 3:16 (KJV):
For God so loved the world, that he gave his only begotten Son, that whosoever believeth in him should not perish, but have everlasting life.

The first point about giving is that it has a motivation. God's motivation was LOVE. He loved everyone in the world. That ocean of love is what prompted his giving. God sent his Son into the world. At that point, he GAVE. He no longer had direct control over the gift. It had "left his hand," so to speak. The second point about the gift is that it had a purpose. The next verse says, **"For God sent not his Son into the world to condemn the world, but that the world through him might be saved."** What a tremendous gift! God sent his Son into the world, not just to be a great teacher, but also to die on the cross for our sins, as the complete sacrifice and offering.

All giving follows this pattern. This is the premise of the lessons of this book. Any giving that we do should follow the example of God, our Father. All giving should be motivated by love and needs to have a purpose, a result that is intended.

ENRICHED IN EVERYTHING

How to use the lessons

Many of the lessons in the book use various translations of the Bible and particular emphasis is given to the study of Aramaic words. Light of the Word Ministry is an organization with a mission to promote the study of the Aramaic Scriptures of the New Testament, as well as Biblical customs and figures of speech, all with the overall goal of adding "light" to our understanding. The verses from the Aramaic translation from the Peshitta that we are working on, as well as information from other books, will give you a preliminary introduction to this type of study. I encourage you to gather as many English translations as you can and to read the passages in several at a time.

This book is the first in a series, called The Searchlight Series. These will be topical studies that are designed to put a "searchlight" on pertinent areas of the Bible, to bring out the great truths in them and to **"open the eyes of our understanding" (Ephesians 1:18)**. There are many books that you can use to accompany the lessons: a good Bible Dictionary, a concordance (for example, either Young's or Strong's), and lexicons for Hebrew and Greek. There are quite a few references listed in the bibliography that will also give you a start with further study.

I suggest if you are using this book for personal study that you get a journal or small notebook to use in conjunction with the study, so that you can notate your thoughts, insights, and questions. This will be wonderful record of the things that you have seen and things you would like to pursue further. If you will be using the book in a discussion group, I would still encourage the group leader to have someone take notes, as well as to have the participants bring their own personal notes. It is amazing what tremendous ideas are generated by a discussion of this nature and you will want to remember what was brought out in the session.

11

SETTING THE PREMISE

The last suggestion is that you read this book with much prayer. Pray for understanding, but also that there be solutions to the application of these lessons in the Church today. There are so many needs in the body of Christ today! I believe that the lessons are timely in providing answers to questions that believers have. Let the light make manifest the darkness of the areas of our lives where we need to change.

Now to begin, write down your own definition of giving. If you like, look up the definition in a dictionary such as Webster's. Then ask yourself several questions and try to formulate as specific an answer as possible. How do you give now? What do you give? What do you want to learn about this topic? What areas of your life would you like to grow in regarding this topic? This will help you to set some goals and will be a place to return to after the completion of the lessons.

Chapter 1
Establishment of the Offering

The first offering recorded in the Bible is from Abel and Cain. It is recorded that **"at the end of days"** (meaning the end of the week) Cain and Abel brought something to the Lord, Yahweh. The phrase, "end of days" might imply that it was on the seventh day, however it appears to be a more general idiom.

> **Genesis 4:2-4 (Original Bible Project translation):**
> **And she continued to bear his brother, Abel. And Abel was a keeper of a flock, but Cain was a worker of *the* ground.**
> **And end of days came and Cain brought an offering to YHVH from the fruit of the ground.**
> **And Abel, he also brought from the firstborn of his flock and from their fat portions. And YHVH looked *favorably* toward Abel and toward his offering;**
> **But toward Cain, and toward his offering he did not look. And Cain burned with anger and his face fell.**

Before we discuss the offering and what it was, we need to go even farther back in Genesis and see why they were bringing an offering at all.

> **Genesis 3:2 (OBP translation):**
> **And YHVH ELOHIM made robes of skin for Adam and his wife, and he clothed them.**

When Adam and Eve sinned, they had been told, **"In the day that you eat thereof, ye shall surely die."** They didn't die that day when God found them in the garden. Why not? I believe that the reason they did not die, was that God told them that it was available for something else to die as a substitution for their sin, so that the sin could be forgiven. That is the reason he made them robes of skin. An animal was slain in the place of Adam and Eve so that they did not die. Then they were given the coats of skin to be a reminder of how they had been forgiven. It was a principle that remains throughout the Word of God:

Hebrews 9:22 (KJV):
Without the shedding of blood, there is no remission.

This principle was unfolded to Adam and Eve and they taught it to their sons, Cain and Abel. The acknowledgement of the substitution for sins was the foundational reason for the offering. Now we can understand why Abel's offering was accepted, but Cain's was not. It is not recorded that Cain gave a poorer offering (not the best fruits) and later on in the Law, it is perfectly acceptable to give of the fruit of the ground as an offering. What he did was fail to acknowledge that he needed forgiveness.

Cain thought he had a better idea than God regarding what would be a good offering. His offering was not accepted by God. In verse 5 of Genesis 4, it says, **"toward his offering he [God] did not look."** God did not even notice that Cain had given an offering. Yet he accepted Abel's offering wholeheartedly. Cain had substituted his own idea of what the offering should be, but then he also refused to change once it was not accepted. Does this sound like so many of us?

Cain burned with anger and his face fell. This is the next temptation mentioned in the Bible, after Adam and Eve's sin:

the temptation to hold to our own thinking and to refuse to change. This temptation is further explained in the passage.

Genesis 4:6-7 (OBP translation):
And YHVH said to Cain, "Why are you burning with anger? And why has your face fallen?
If you do well, *there is* a lifting up, but if you do not do well, sin is an evil influence at the door and its desire *is* for you, but you must rule over it.

Sin is pictured here in the Hebrew like a lion crouching to overcome its prey. The Rabbinic interpretation understands the masculine "it" as a reference to an "evil inclination." "Sin is an evil influence at the door" is a great translation of the difficult Hebrew passage.[1] If Cain had done well, his offering would have been accepted. Because he did not, he let the sin come and pounce on him as prey and he was overcome by it. This led to the murder of Abel, because Cain refused to change and continued to think that he was right. He failed to take responsibility for his own actions, seek to be forgiven, but instead, blamed someone else for his own faults. Does this sound typical of our human tendency?

Abel understood that the first lesson of worshipping God was to be obedient, rather than to do what **he** thought might be good. It was his faith that was accepted by God because he acknowledged that God was the source of his righteousness. Righteousness here means simply a right standing with God. Hebrews states this succinctly and uses Abel as the first example of faith:

Hebrews 11:4 (Bullinger):
By faith Abel offered unto God a more excellent sacrifice than Cain by which he obtained witness

---

[1] The Original Bible Project, Preliminary Edition, *The Book of Genesis*, p. 10.

that he was righteous, God Himself bearing witness to his gifts: and by it [i.e., by means of his faith which led to his martyrdom] **he, having died, yet speaketh.** [2]

Abel, on the other hand, went beyond the original unfolding of the sacrifice for the forgiveness of sins, and understood that it was important to give of the FIRSTBORN of the flock and from the fat portions. It is not indicated in the text whether he received this as revelation from Yahweh or not, but it is the outward show that his heart was to honor God with the best that he had. This is also more important than just that Abel gave of his best from his flock. He understood that the offering was pointing to what the Lord Jesus Christ was going to do to provide salvation.

Jesus had to die so that his blood would be shed for the sins of mankind. He was the complete substitute. He was the firstborn and the best sacrifice because he was God's only-begotten Son. The first offering is the acknowledgement of this provision that God was going to make for mankind.

Then it was for God to give his testimony that He had accepted it. We do not earn the acceptance of God because of our offering. The offering only represents what we believe about the substitution of Jesus for our sins. God pronounces us righteous and accepts us only in the person of Jesus Christ. Why? Because God accepted the once and final offering when He raised Jesus from the dead. That was the acceptance, just as He accepted Abel's offering.

E.W. Bullinger sums up this point with these words: "Abel believed God, and he was judicially acquitted. God bore witness to his gifts by accepting the death of the substituted lamb, instead of the death that Abel deserved as a sinner.

---

[2] Bullinger, <u>Great Cloud of Witnesses</u>, p. 32.

Hence Abel was righteous; and stood judicially acquitted before God." [3]

We can now take this and learn the lessons regarding offering. There is nothing that we have of ourselves that is good enough to present to God. Abel understood this and that is why he is a great example of faith. We have an offering accepted by God because of 1) obedience, and 2) faith. Only in obedience to His revelation will there be an acceptance of the offering and also of the one offering. Only when we keep in mind the finished work of Jesus Christ and that He only is the complete sacrifice for our sins, will any offering be accepted. These points are very humbling. May God continue to show us how to apply them in our own lives.

Study Questions

1) What are reasons for using animals for offerings? What principle is the foundation for the first offering?
2) Consider why Cain did not repent and just change his offering. What is the lesson to learn for us today?
3) Think of at least one way that we can honor God with the best that we have. Write down some examples of times that you were obedient to what God said to give and times that you were not.
4) How is Abel an example of faith? What is the relationship of faith with obedience?

---

[3] Bullinger, Great Cloud of Witnesses, p. 65.

Chapter 2
Abram and Lot

The story of Abram and the first giving of a tithe is a study in contradictions. The two main sets of opposites are Abram and Lot, and the king of Sodom and the king of Salem. Let's review the events leading up to the incident in Genesis 14.

Abram and Lot had parted company in chapter 13, when Abram had given Lot the choice of which district he wanted to live in. Lot chose to go eastward from Bethel to the tropical valley and fertile region called the "circle of Jordan" to the north of the Dead Sea.

> **Genesis 13:10, 11 (Original Bible Project translation):**
> **And Lot lifted up his eyes, and he saw the whole circuit of the Jordan, that it *was* well watered everywhere (before YHVH destroyed Sodom and Gomorrah), like the garden of YHVH, like the land of Egypt, when you come to Zoar.**
> **And Lot chose for himself all the circuit of the Jordan, and Lot journeyed east; and they were separated, one from the other.**

Lot saw this beautiful, well-watered area and his heart went toward it, unmindful of what kind of inhabitants lived there. Verse 11 says that HE CHOSE. It was not necessarily what God wanted for him. At first in verse 12, Lot moved his tent only NEAR Sodom. Later, just before the destruction of Sodom and Gomorrah, we find him living in the city and actually "sitting in the gate" as one of the elders of the city leadership (Genesis 19:1).

ENRICHED IN EVERYTHING

The first contrast in these chapters between Abram and Lot shows Abram's stand of faith and trust in God's direction and Lot's quest for riches, wealth, and ease. Whenever we go toward the world's way of gathering riches and ease of life, we are subject to being corrupted by the sin of that "city," so to speak. Lot never completely succumbed to the evil of the city. However when Sodom was utterly destroyed, he lost his wealth and his wife and household.

The Rescue of Lot

Sometime prior to the destruction of Sodom, Lot and his whole family are taken captive with the other inhabitants of the city when they are caught up in a war between five kings of the local cities and four kings of the Elamites (the Babylonian area). For twelve years the kings of the Jordan River "circuit" had served Chedorlaomer (of the descendants of Nimrod). In the thirteenth year of their subjugation, the Canaanite kings rebelled. In the fourteenth year, Chedorlaomer came with three allies to invade them. Chedorlaomer was very successful in the campaign, Sodom and Gomorrah were plundered, and in the process, Lot and all his family were taken captive.

Since Chedorlaomer and his allies had come all the way from Babylonia, they surely had no small entourage, with the soldiers, baggage, and now all the spoils of their victory. Abram pursued the victors with 318 of his own trained servants and men from the district around Hebron, but it was not a great army. It is interesting that very little description is made in this record of HOW Abram defeated this powerful alliance of kings with such a small band. The omission of this description speaks very loudly that the only way Abram could have routed this army was that God helped him in every detail. Abram's stand of faith and trust in Jehovah (or Yahweh) as God in relation to His people made it easy to defeat the Elamites and bring back all the possessions that had been taken. The record reminds us of many other times in the Old

19

Testament when the Israelites won victories with a small force, just because God was on their side.

The Blessing of Melchizedek

Now we have another study in contrasts as Abram returned with Lot and all the spoils taken from Sodom and Gomorrah. Abram is met in the "Valley of the King" (near what would be known as Jerusalem) by two people with very different characters. Abram's actions toward each of these men show his faith again.

The first man who went up to meet Abram is the new king of Sodom. His predecessor had fallen in the battle with Chedorlaomer. The second man is Melchizedek, the king of Salem. Salem is the ancient Jerusalem. This Melchizedek was a combination of priest and king and served the Most High God, El Elyon. Abram received a blessing from Melchizedek and gave him a tenth of "everything" of the spoil. The king of Sodom wanted to thank Abram for bringing everything back, so he offered Abram all the spoils, but Abram immediately rebuffed him and refused to take anything from him, so that he would not be tied or beholden to him in any way. All the way along during this meeting we can see Abram walking with God and doing what God wanted.

Melchizedek has been the topic of much speculation throughout the centuries, but it is primarily because he has no genealogy and no records exist regarding where he came from. God did not record his genealogy intentionally, because he is a type of the Messiah and foreshadows the combination of the office of priest and king in one man, our Lord Jesus Christ. These explanations are found in Psalm 110:4 and Hebrews 7:3.

The contrast between the responses of Abram to the two kings is that from the one, he takes nothing, and to the other, he gives a tenth. In this chapter, we are studying this first record of giving a tenth to see what the foundational principles are of giving. The key to this passage is in the blessing of Abram by Melchizedek.

> **Genesis 14:19, 20 (KJV):**
> **And he blessed him, and said, "Blessed _be_ Abram of the most high God, possessor of heaven and earth;**
> **And blessed be the most high God, which hath delivered thine enemies into thy hand." And he gave him tithes of all.**

God Most High is the possessor of the heavens and the earth. Melchizedek's authority as priest rested in God Most High as the source of all possessions and deliverance. "Possessor" is the Hebrew word _qanah_ and the Aramaic verb _qena_. This is one of the words that can be worked in both the Old and New Testaments, because of the close relationship with the languages. _Qena_ means to acquire, purchase or obtain, thus to possess. In a sense, God purchased the earth and all its wealth, when He made it during the days of creation. The noun that is derived from _qena_ in Aramaic is _qenina_ and can be translated wealth, possession, or property.

In the Eastern concept of ownership, wealth was definitely measured by the number of possessions one had.[4] One Hebrew noun derived from _qanah_ is _miqueh,_ and primarily means possessions. It is also the term for cattle or oxen. "So much of the wealth of early Hebrews consisted of herds and flocks that the same term was used to designate 'possessions' and 'cattle.'"[5] From this brief study of _qena_, we conclude that Melchizedek's blessing on Abram acknowledged the Most High God as the source of all wealth and possessions.

Abram echoes this acknowledgement in verse 22 and adds his special relationship with Jehovah to the name El Elyon.

---

[4] Other references to study: Matt 19:21; Luke 8:42, 16:1; Acts 2:45.
[5] Rice, <u>Orientalisms in Bible Lands</u>, p. 176.

ABRAM AND LOT

Genesis 14:22 (KJV):
And Abram said to the king of Sodom, I have lift
up my hand unto the Lord, the most high God, the
possessor of heaven and earth,

There is another part of the blessing of Melchizedek that we need to note here from verse 20. The Most High God is also the source of all deliverance from enemies. Deliver is the Hebrew word *magan*. It also has a related Aramaic word, *magan*, that is used in Romans 3:24 for the word "freely." It means to cover, give freely. The noun in Hebrew derived from it means shield or buckler. God delivered Abram's enemies, or gave them freely, into his hand. The verse in Romans says that we are justified freely (or without a cause). The cause of the deliverance to Abram had everything to do with Abram's relationship with Jehovah. God brought the victory to pass, as we saw from the review of the story.

Now we can ask the question, what was the purpose of the giving of the tenth? There were two reasons that Abram gave the tenth to Melchizedek as the representative of the Most High God: 1) to acknowledge that God was the source and holder of all wealth and acquisition, and 2) to show that his victory over his enemies came because of God's deliverance. These two reasons are the foundation for the law of the tithe that was established later, as well as the foundation of all application of the giving of the tenth in our lives today.

Every offering we give to a church or representative of God should first be done with obedience to God's will (as we saw in chapter one) and then as an acknowledgement that God is the source of all our wealth and deliverance. The two aspects of wealth and deliverance are very important. It is very easy when we do have wealth and possessions to think that our deliverance comes by our own hand. Abram never counted on his property to accomplish this. He knew that God, who is the Highest, or Most High, was the one who had called him and given him the promises, and only HE could bring them to pass.

When God promises us that He will **"supply all our need according to his riches in glory by Christ Jesus"** (Philippians 4:13), we see that it is the same as Abram. Which man do you want to be like, Abram or Lot?

Study Questions

1) List several character traits that are exhibited by Abram in one column and Lot in another. Compare and contrast other points that are not mentioned in the article.
2) List reasons you think that Lot chose to go towards Sodom. Think of some of the temptations that faced him in that city.
3) If God is the holder of all possessions, that includes yours and mine. Are there any of your "possessions" that you need to give back to Him? How could that be demonstrated?
4) Why did Abram not accept the spoils of the battle from the king of Sodom? Were there any other battles in the Old Testament where they did not keep the spoils for similar reasons?
5) How did Abram get all his wealth? In what way is he a good example of maintaining his integrity despite having wealth?

Chapter 3
Manna--What Is It?

Manna was the basic food of the Israelites during their wilderness wanderings. It was a miraculous provision that came six days out of seven for almost forty years. The manna teaches us another wonderful lesson regarding giving and again points our hearts toward the true bread from heaven, our Lord Jesus Christ.

After the children of Israel left Egypt, miracle after miracle happened that showed how God was taking care of them. First, Israel walked over the Red Sea on dry land, and then the whole Egyptian army drowned. The pillar of fire by night and cloud by day guided them, and bitter waters were turned sweet at Marah. After that, they found an oasis in the wilderness with twelve wells of water—enough for all the people. But by the middle of the second month after leaving Egypt, the people had run out of food and were complaining very loudly about it. The first thing they wanted to do was to go back to Egypt into bondage, because at least there they had food to eat. How quickly they forgot the true circumstances they had left behind!

The Lord told Moses what He was going to do.

Exodus 16:4 (KJV):
Then said the Lord unto Moses, Behold, I will rain bread from heaven for you; and the people shall go out and gather a certain rate every day, that I may prove them, whether they will walk in my law, or no.

Every morning there was going to be **bread from heaven** for everyone to eat. What a wonderful provision! In the middle of the wilderness, there would be enough food for a million

24

people or more. Can you imagine trying to feed that many people at one time in your city?

Exodus 16:15 (KJV):
And when the children of Israel saw *it*, they said one to another, It *is* manna: for they wist not what it *was*. And Moses said unto them, This is the bread which the Lord hath given you to eat.

The children of Israel did not know what the food was, so they called it *man-ho*, which means, WHAT IS IT? This substance was so unusual. When the dew came in the morning, there was a small round thing left lying on the ground (Exodus 16:14). It had to be gathered early, before the sun became so hot as to melt it. The interesting part about this manna was that it had to be gathered every day and you could only gather enough for one day at a time. To attempt to gather and keep enough for two days failed because it would become wormy and offensive. The only day that it kept overnight was on the day before the Sabbath, so that they would not have to gather it on the Sabbath. It could be prepared by grinding, boiling, baking. In another verse its description is "like coriander seed, white; and the taste of it was like wafers *made* with honey" (Exodus 16:31).

Many people have tried to figure out what kind of natural substance this might have been. There is a kind of white, sweet, residue that is produced by a thorny bush. And also the Bedouins still eat a white substance that is produced by insects. But these substances are not the manna that Israel gathered during the forty years in the wilderness.

The reason I know that it was not a natural substance is from the description of it in Psalms.

Psalm 78:24, 25 (KJV):
And had rained down manna upon them to eat, and had given them of the corn of heaven.

MANNA – WHAT IS IT?

Man did eat angel's food: he sent them meat to the full.

In Exodus it is called "bread from heaven," in Psalms, "corn from heaven," and "angel's food." That's not angel's food cake, but literally means, "bread of the mighty." [6]

This miraculous provision continued every week for all the time Israel was in the wilderness. It stopped on the day after they had crossed over the Jordan and started eating the corn in the land of Canaan (Joshua 5:12). What was the lesson of the manna? The first verse that we read in this chapter said that the Lord gave the manna **"that I may prove them, whether they will walk in my law, or no."** Deuteronomy continues to explain this "proving."

Deuteronomy 8:3 9 (KJV):
And he humbled thee, and suffered thee to hunger, and fed thee with manna, which thou knewest not, neither did thy fathers know; that he might make thee know that man doth not live by bread only, but by every *word* that proceedeth out of the mouth of the Lord doth man live.

The purpose of the manna was twofold: 1) to teach Israel to depend on God for daily provision, and 2) to realize that true bread is spiritual and that is the only kind that brings life. The manna came every day in the morning. Israel had to trust that the next day it would come again. They couldn't "save up for a rainy day." It made them dependent on God DAILY. Even in the Lord's Prayer, Jesus taught his disciples to pray, **"Give us this day our daily bread."** The Aramaic of Matthew 6:11 says, **"Give us the bread of our need day by day."** Each day we need to trust that God will provide what we need THAT DAY.

---

[6] Theological Wordbook of the Old Testament, p. 512.

The second purpose of the giving of the manna was to teach the Israelites that true bread is spiritual, not physical. The manna was not something they were familiar with and it was not a natural substance. They could not procure it for themselves. This purpose is explained further on in the passage in Deuteronomy.

Deuteronomy 8:16-18 9 (KJV):
Who fed thee in the wilderness with manna, which thy fathers knew not, that he might humble thee, and that he might prove thee, to do thee good at thy latter end;
And thou say in thine heart, My power and the might of *mine* hand hath gotten me this wealth.
But thou shalt remember the Lord thy God: for *it is* he that giveth thee power to get wealth, that he may establish his covenant which he sware unto thy fathers, as *it is* this day.

The purpose of the daily manna was to **prove** Israel and humble them. They could not provide bread for themselves in the wilderness and so it was a daily reminder that spiritual bread was the most important. It is the Lord God who gives power to get wealth and the giving of wealth is to establish His covenant. Part of the covenant was that God would take care of His people. The other part was that it was a spiritual relationship.

Jesus further clarifies this aspect of spiritual bread in John 6. The true bread is spoken of as coming from heaven seven times in this chapter.

John 6:32-33 (NIV):
Jesus said to them: I tell you the truth, it is not Moses who has given you the bread from heaven; but it is my Father who gives you the true bread from heaven.

MANNA – WHAT IS IT?

For the bread of God is he who comes down from heaven and gives life to the world.

Jesus explained that he was the bread of life and the **"bread that came down from heaven"** (vs. 41). The Jews had a hard time understanding this, even as they did in the wilderness. Also, we as Christians today do not understand that our spiritual sustenance is more important than the physical.

John 6:46-51 (NIV):
No one has seen the Father except the one who is from God; only he has seen the Father.
I tell you the truth, he who believes has everlasting life.
I am the bread of life.
Your forefathers ate the manna in the desert, yet they died.
But here is the bread that comes down from heaven, which a man may eat and not die.
I am the living bread that came down from heaven. If anyone eats of this bread, he will live forever. This bread is my flesh, which I will give for the life of the world.

The manna in the wilderness was a picture of the true "heavenly provision" of God, which would be his Son, Jesus. He who eats this bread lives forever. All the provision of God points to his Son and the spiritual life available from him.

Manna—what is it? It is not by our own power that we get wealth. It is always by a heavenly provision! Whether we acknowledge that it has come from God—or not—determines whether we will have life from it—or not. That was the proving of the children of Israel in the wilderness and it is our proving today. Do you believe that you have life from your job, from your own work? Or do you see that all life comes from the Lord God and it is His daily provision that allows you to have the things you need? Do you see that spiritual food, i.e. our relationship with the Lord Jesus Christ, is what brings life?

Study Questions

1) What is the manna? What did it look like? Do you think the children of Israel would have tired of eating it? How was it prepared?
2) Can you think of examples of God giving you this kind of **daily** provision?
3) What was the temptation in the gospels when Jesus quoted Deuteronomy 8:3: **"Man shall not live by bread alone…?"**
4) Explain how Jesus is the true bread from heaven and what that means for you.

Chapter 4
The Principle of First Fruits

In the church today, there is much argument regarding tithes and offerings. All one needs to do is to go on the Internet to see the range of arguments for and against applying the Old Covenant laws to the church today. Rather than take a strict stand for or against one of these arguments, the next two chapters will be a study of the principles regarding first fruits, tithes, and offerings. This study will give you the background that will help you to decide for yourself what the application is for today. The premise that I, as the author, use to approach this subject is that interpretation and application of the Scriptures must be done in light of to whom it is written. Then further application to this present time must be done in light of principles, which are unchanging from one time period to another. This will become apparent as we progress in this study.

The first principle to investigate is the principle regarding first fruits. During the giving of the Law, God set up the application of a principle that was already in common practice in the Near East. That principle was that the firstborn and first of the harvest belonged to God, and should be presented to Him as an offering or sacrifice. This offering or sacrifice was a redemption, or buying back, of the rest of the increase in the fields and of the flocks and herds. By returning a portion to God and acknowledging that He was the source of the increase, the balance of the increase became available for human use. The offerings of the agricultural crops were known as first fruits and the offerings of the animals to be sacrificed were called firstlings.

The very first of the ordinances that God revealed to Moses after the children of Israel came out of Egypt was to dedicate to God the firstborn of all children and animals.

Exodus 13:2, 11-13 (KJV):
Sanctify unto me all the firstborn, whatsoever openeth the womb among the children of Israel, *both* **of man and of beast: it** *is* **mine.**
And it shall be when the Lord shall bring thee into the land of the Canaanites, as he sware unto thee and to thy fathers, and shall give it thee,
That thou shalt set apart unto the Lord all that openeth the matrix, and every firstling that cometh of a beast which thou hast; the males *shall be* **the Lord's.**
And every firstling of an ass thou shalt redeem with a lamb; and if thou wilt not redeem it, then thou shalt break his neck: and all the firstborn of man among thy children shalt thou redeem.

Why was this so important that it was the first revelation to Moses after the captivity?

Exodus 13:14-16 9 (KJV):
And it shall be when thy son asketh thee in time to come, saying, What *is* **this? That thou shalt say unto him, By strength of hand the Lord brought us out from Egypt, from the house of bondage:**
And it came to pass, when Pharaoh would hardly let us go, that the Lord slew all the firstborn in the land of Egypt, both the firstborn of man, and the firstborn of beast: therefore I sacrifice to the Lord all that openeth the matrix, being males; but all the firstborn of my children I redeem.

And it shall be for a token upon thine hand, and for frontlets between thine eyes: for by strength of hand the Lord brought us forth out of Egypt.

The dedication of the firstborn of both animals and man was to be a token or sign of the deliverance that was performed by God in bringing Israel out of bondage.

If we understood this principle, then the application is pertinent to the church today also. Before we talk about anything with tithes and offerings, we need to dedicate our firstborn children, and especially sons, to God. This is an acknowledgement of the redemption from bondage to death, which is symbolized to us also by the ending of the captivity of Egypt (see Romans 8:15). How did they dedicate their firstborn children? Obviously, it was not God's will that they actually sacrifice them on an altar as some other cultures did (for example Moab and Ammon). This brings us to the study of the passage in this chapter.

At the time that the Lord talked with Moses on Mount Sinai, he told Moses that Aaron and his family would be the priests for the children of Israel. Further, he told him that the whole tribe of Levi would be dedicated to serve the rest of Israel.

Numbers 3:5-9 (NIV):
The Lord said to Moses,
"Bring the tribe of Levi and present them to Aaron the priest to assist him.
They are to perform duties for him and for the whole community at the Tent of Meeting by doing the work of the tabernacle.
They are to take care of all the furnishings of the Tent of Meeting, fulfilling the obligations of the Israelites by doing the work of the tabernacle.
Give the Levites to Aaron and his sons; they are the Israelites who are to be given wholly to him.

This dedication of the tribe of Levi was to take the place of the firstborn of Israel.

Numbers 3:11-13 (NIV):
The Lord also said to Moses,
"I have taken the Levites from among the Israelites in place of the first male offspring of every Israelite woman. The Levites are mine,
for all the firstborn are mine. When I struck down all the firstborn in Egypt, I set apart for myself every firstborn in Israel, whether man or animal. They are to be mine. I am the Lord."

Then the Lord told Moses to count all the Levites by their families and clans. The numbers of each family and clan are listed verses 17-39. The total was 22,000 males from one month old and upward. Then the Lord told Moses to number all the firstborn Israelite males who were a month old or more. That total number was 22,273. The difference of 273 males was to be redeemed with five shekels each.

Numbers 3:46-51:
To redeem the 273 firstborn Israelites who exceed the number of the Levites,
Collect five shekels for each one, according to the sanctuary shekel, which weighs twenty gerahs.
Give the money for the redemption of the additional Israelites to Aaron and his sons."
So Moses collected the redemption money from those who exceeded the number redeemed by the Levites.
From the firstborn of the Israelites he collected silver weighing 1,365 shekels, according to the sanctuary shekel.

Moses gave the redemption money to Aaron and his sons, as he was commanded by the word of the Lord.

This difference of 1,365 shekels was equal to 35 pounds of silver. That would be roughly equivalent in the year 2000 to $2,800, with silver valued at $5.00 an ounce. Also, the livestock of the Levites was taken in lieu of all the livestock of the Israelites. It does not say that there was a counting for this.

In Jeremiah 2:3, it describes another perspective of this principle of firstfruits. **"Israel was holiness unto the Lord, and the first fruits of his increase."** That is also why Aaron wore a plate of pure gold that had "Holiness to the Lord" engraved on it (Exodus 28:36-38). The setting apart of the Levites, and specifically the family of Aaron, was to dedicate them to God as holy. They were to perform God's work and to serve all the rest of the community of Israel. This parallel in our day and time can be seen in that the whole church of the body is a "royal priesthood," dedicated to serving the community of the people of the world with the Gospel and to show forth praises to God (I Peter 2:9). Like the firstborn of man and animal, the first fruits were holy to God. They were given to the priests.

Deuteronomy 18:3-5 (KJV):
And this shall be the priest's due from the people, from them that offer a sacrifice, whether *it be* ox or sheep; and they shall give unto the priest the shoulder, and the two cheeks, and the maw.
The firstfruit *also* of thy corn, of thy wine, and of thine oil, and the first of the fleece of thy sheep, shalt thou give him.
For the Lord thy God hath chosen him out of all thy tribes, to stand to minister in the name of the Lord, him and his sons for ever.

Two-fold purpose of the first fruits

The offering of the first fruits of the soil was incorporated into the ordinances regarding the celebration of Passover, Pentecost, and Tabernacles. These three were annual pilgrimage festivals at which all men were to appear before the Lord God. They were not to appear empty handed, but were to bring the best of the first fruits of the soil to the house of God. These feasts revolved around the various harvests of barley, wheat, and fruit. There was a public offering of the first sheaf of the barley harvest at Passover before the commencement of the grain harvest (see Leviticus 23:10, 11). Then, at Pentecost, the two loaves offered were made of the new flour from the harvest and were offered when the harvest was completed. The Feast of Tabernacles was celebrated after the ingathering of the harvest and fruits. Living in booths or tents during this festival represented the time during the wilderness when they lived in tents, and was a reminder of God's loving care in the wilderness. It was a reminder of his continuing care during the year and that he was the source of their prosperity. One could do an extensive study just on the meaning of the feasts and their fulfillment in Christ. But even from this brief explanation, it is easy to see that the purpose of the giving of the first fruits was a combination of thankfulness to God for the harvest and a provision for the priests who ministered to the people.

This two-fold purpose of the giving of first fruits, whether it is of animals or produce, should be the foundation for all discussion of application to the Church today. God says that the firstborn, the firstlings, and the first fruits all belong to him. They are holy to the Lord. In order for us to use them, they must either be redeemed by other animals, or redeemed with money. The system of tithing and offerings under the Law was set up to regulate this process of redemption. No matter how they are redeemed, the part that is unchanging is that they belong to God. They are a testimony that God redeemed

Israel (and us too) from the bondage of Egypt (our sin) and continues to provide for our every need in every category.

I believe that there should be more teaching in the Church today on the subject of dedication of the firstborn children to God, especially male children. I learned this principle several years ago and at that time, my firstborn son was going through some struggles in school and did not have any direction in his life. In a simple process of dedication, as well as by a special gift, which only God knew about, I gave his life to God. Since that time, his life has taken a total turn-around. He has made specific decisions about the direction of his life, his outlook toward God and others has changed (for the better), and I am eagerly looking forward to how God will continue to work in his life.

As far as the application of this principle to our lives today, not living in an agricultural society, it does not seem to be difficult to apply how this would work for our lives, as workers in and owners of companies. Why would our society be any different as far as the principles of God are concerned? The principles stay the same; only the application is different. There are many people who "tithe," but who do not have any idea about what they are doing or why they give to a particular church or minister. Gift ministers in the church today are the "set apart ones" like the priests were to Israel. Church leaders and organizational leaders play a similar role to the Levites as they minister in the affairs of the church to the whole community. The reason to give to any minister or Church has to be based on what their function is in the body of Christ and if they are not truly functioning in the body then perhaps you should give to someone who is. And even if one gives, but only does so after all his other bills are paid, or after seeing "how much he has left," he does not understand that this principle of first fruits is what is **"holy to the Lord." "He that hath ears to hear, let him hear."** We will discuss the specific tithes and offerings in the next chapter.

Study Questions

1) Consider the situation in your own life regarding the dedication of the firstborn. What did you do (baptism, dedication, etc) of your child as an infant? Was there an accompanying offering? What could you do now? Can you think of examples of other families if you do not have children of your own, where the parents did dedicate their children to God and this has made a difference?

2) What would you consider as the firstlings and first fruits of your particular life?

3) Can you think of any examples in Samuel through Chronicles where the kings initiated a renewal of the celebration of the feasts and there was tremendous rejoicing over the acknowledgement of Jehovah as the provider of the harvest?

4) Consider the comparison of how Christ is the "first fruits of them that slept" (I Corinthians 15:20-23). How does that fit with being holy to the Lord?

5) Do a word study on all of the uses of the term "first fruits" in both the Old and New Testaments and add any further insights to your understanding of the principle (Hebrew: *raysheeth bikkoor* and Greek: *aparche*).

Chapter 5
Don't Cheat

There are many aspects of tithes and offerings that could be studied. In fact in the bibliography there are several books listed that pertain to the study of the types that the offerings foreshadow about Christ. He was the perfect offering and fulfilled the Old Testament system of sacrifice in every detail. However, the lesson of this chapter is "don't cheat!" It is part of all of the records that have to do with tithes and offerings in the Old Testament. We will look at some of the details about the Law, but see how this principle glares out at us through all the description.

Leviticus 27 should be read by every person who believes in the tithe's application to the Church today.

Leviticus 27:30-34 (NIV):
"A tithe of everything from the land, whether grain from the soil or fruit from the trees, belongs to the Lord; it is holy to the Lord.
If a man redeems any of his tithe, he must add a fifth of the value to it.
The entire tithe of the herd and flock—every tenth animal that passes under the shepherd's rod—will be holy to the Lord.
He must not pick out the good from the bad or make any substitution. If he does make a substitution, both the animal and its substitute become holy and cannot be redeemed."

38

In the previous chapter, we discussed the principle of first fruits. This must not be confused with tithing. Tithing means to "take the tenth part." The tenth part of all the produce and animals belonged to God. The agricultural portion of the tithe could be redeemed by adding 20% or 1/5 to the value of the tithe. There was no such exchange for animals. If someone tried to substitute another animal for the one that came under the rod, both animals were to be given to God.

The tithes were given to the Levites, who in turn were to give 1/10 to the priests for the service of the temple. Then every third year, this extra 1/10 was to remain in the local communities and be distributed by way of a grand feast to the poor. The Levites were to give the best portion of the tithes to the priests.

Numbers 18:28 (KJV):
Thus ye also shall offer an heave offering unto the Lord of all your tithes, which ye receive of the children of Israel; and ye shall give thereof the Lord's heave offering to Aaron the priest.

The Levites could use the tithes for their own living and for their families only after they had given the best to the priests. There was a very harsh punishment if they did not do this:

Numbers 18:32 (KJV):
And ye shall bear no sin by reason of it, when ye have heaved from it the best of it: neither shall ye pollute the holy things of the children of Israel, lest ye die.

So already we see that there is much temptation to "cheat." The people could cheat by not redeeming the agricultural produce, by not adding the extra 20%, or by not giving it to the Levites to begin with. The children of Israel did all of these things for many years at a time and withheld the support of the Levites and the priests. The Levites could cheat by not giving the tenth of the tenth to the priests and withholding the best of the tithe for themselves. This resulted in the poverty of the priests who ministered exclusively in the service of the Temple. In addition, the Levites could cheat by not taking the tithe every third year to provide for the poor.

Cheating was a temptation regarding the offerings as well. The system of tithing was only one portion of the way that God provided for the priests. The first fruit offerings and the other sacrificial offerings were also to be shared with the priests. There were five main offerings besides the first fruits and specific portions belonged to the priests. This proscription is detailed in Leviticus chapters 6 and 7.

1) Burnt offering
This offering was the only one that was burnt wholly on the altar. No portion of the meat was given to the priests, only the skin.

2) Sin offering
This offering was offered for payment for sin and the blood of the offering was sprinkled at the door of the veil and upon the horns of the altar and at the bottom of the altar. The fat portions of the animal were burned on the altar. The skin was given to the priests as well as the rest of the meat. The priests were able to eat the meat in a holy place, in the courtyard of the Tabernacle and Temple. And any male in the priest's family could eat it.

3) Trespass offering
This offering was given for specific cases of wrongdoing and made restitution for the person committing the offense. The priest's portion was the same as in the sin offering.

4) Meal offering

This offering accompanied the sin and trespass offerings, as well as the peace offerings. It was made up of fine flour, frankincense, oil and salt. A handful of the meal, part of the oil, and all the frankincense, were laid on the altar. All the remainder was given to the priests. The table of the showbread was given to the priests after it had been replaced on the seventh day.

5) Peace offering

There were three kinds of peace offerings: thank offerings, vow offerings, and freewill offerings. They were given for specific instances of thankfulness for God's mercies in a person's life, such as festivals, birth of a child, fulfillment of a vow, or any other specific times of thankfulness. These peace offerings were the only offerings in which the offerer was allowed to share. The fat was burned on the altar and the heave-shoulder and the wave-breast were given to the priests. The rest belonged to the one making the offering, so that he could share with his friends and family in the rejoicing.

This is a very brief overview of the offerings. There were specific laws regarding the animals to be sacrificed for each, methods of killing the animals, and the particular way that the priests handled each kind. Christ is our offering for sin, and as Hebrews 10:14 states, **"For by one offering he hath perfected for ever them that are sanctified."** We no longer have need of sacrifices, for our high priest has completed the system of offerings in every fashion.

However, the idea of the peace offering is still with us, not in the actual burning on the altar, but in the aspect of sharing with the priests or ministers of the things of the service of the temple. Whenever we have a church potluck, share in a dinner of rejoicing for something we have had happen in our lives, or give a gift because of God's special mercies in our lives, these are "peace offerings."

In all these offerings, it was available to cheat. One could bring a blemished animal for the burnt offering. One could bring wormy meal or second rate flour for the meal offering. One could bring a lesser animal than required for the offering. The priests could take more than their share and refuse to burn the fat portions on the altar. This was the case during the time of Eli the High Priest, whose sons were taking more than their share. In the case of a vow offering, the person could choose not to fulfill the vow, when the request he had made came to pass. Hannah did not do this when she had vowed to dedicate her first child to God if he would open her womb. That is how Samuel came to be a minister in the temple with Eli.

One of the best examples of cheating in the New Testament is that of Ananias and Sapphira. In Acts 5, both of them die because they were not honest about the gift that they brought to the apostles. It had nothing to do with whether they were required to bring the gift. It was that they cheated about the price of the land and were not honest in their presentation.

We could discuss for hours how to apply the different aspects of the tithes and offerings. It is not the intention of this book that we should mandate one way or another, for as the further chapters will show, we believe that in the Church today that there is strictly a freewill choice about what to give. But as we do endeavor to apply the principles of the Old Testament, it is important to note several points. The total amount that was given to the Levites was more than 10% of one's income. There were special tithes for the poor. Also, the Levites were required to give the tenth of a tenth to the priests and this was to be the best share. The offerings were above and beyond the tithes and first fruits and were given to the priests. The main purpose of all of these types of giving was to provide for the Levites, the priests, and the poor.

Study Questions

1) Consider how the types of offerings line up with the principles in previous chapters. Which kind of offering did Abel give? What did Abraham practice?
2) What was the purpose of the peace offerings and how can they be applied in your particular fellowship or church?
3) Search your heart for times when you have "cheated." What were you trying to gain or avoid? Confess the unrighteousness, repent, and make plans to do right in the future.
4) How does cheating affect the flow of blessings from God from your giving? What can you do to change this?

Chapter 6
What is True Prosperity?

Our culture idolizes "being successful." Status is everything! It is determined by the car you drive, the house you live in, the job you have, if you went to the right school, if your husband/wife is beautiful, and if you are beautiful, just to name a few criteria. "Beauty, brains and bucks" are the goals of many people. But what is true success or prosperity? The only way to evaluate whether a person is successful or not should be by looking at what God's view of prosperity is and not the world's view. This study will approach this question by examining the life of Hezekiah.

The Hebrew word for "to prosper" is *tzaleack*. It basically means, "to accomplish satisfactorily what is intended." There is a wonderful statement following this definition in the *Theological Wordbook of the Old Testament* that is worthwhile pondering at this point: "Real prosperity results from the work of God in the life of one who seeks God with all his heart." [7] There are several men in the Old Testament who exemplify God's idea of prosperity. One of them is Joseph. When Joseph began to work for Potiphar, he was diligent about his duties, even though he was a slave. Whatever Joseph found to do, he did with all his might (Ecclesiastes 9:10). The testimony regarding his success is in Genesis 39:

Genesis 39:2-4 (NIV):
The Lord was with Joseph and he prospered, and he lived in the house of his Egyptian master.

---

[7] *Theological Wordbook of the Old Testament*, Vol. II, p. 766.

When his master saw that the Lord was with him and that the Lord gave him success in everything he did,
Joseph found favor in his eyes and became his attendant. Potiphar put him in charge of his household and he entrusted to his care everything he owned.

Joseph's diligence to do what was right, God's will not his own, eventually led to his being placed in the highest position in the land of Egypt, second only to Pharaoh himself.

Another man who is said to have prospered is Uzziah. In II Chronicles 26:5, it says, **"As long as he [Uzziah] sought the Lord, God made him to prosper."** Later in his life, you can read about how his heart was lifted up and he decided to go into the temple to burn incense on the altar, which only the priests were allowed to do, and he was struck with leprosy for the rest of his life. This shows that prosperity is not something one necessarily retains. Uzziah's "success" was very evident in the beginning of his reign. But God's blessing can end by having a **"heart lifted up to his destruction"** (verse 16) and by considering that the prosperity comes from one's own works and greatness. The prosperity comes as a blessing from God because of meekness of heart and seeking God.

The greatest example in the Old Testament of these principles is the story of Hezekiah's life. You can read the whole history of Hezekiah in II Chronicles 29-32, II Kings 18-20, and Isaiah 36-39. Hezekiah was twenty-five years old when he became king and **"he did what was right in the eyes of the Lord, just as his father David had done"** (II Chronicles 29:2). He went through a series of trials with the Assyrians, and after Hezekiah **"cried out in prayer to heaven about this,"** (II Chronicles 32:20) God sent an angel who wiped out 185,000 soldiers of the Assyrian army overnight (II Kings 19:35). Later in his reign, Hezekiah had not had any children yet, and he was very sick and near death. Because he turned his heart back to God, God granted him 15 more years of life. During that time, he had a son and accomplished one of the greatest engineering feats of the world. He built an aqueduct system for Jerusalem, which is still standing today. II Chronicles 32:30 documents that **"he succeeded in everything he undertook."**

The reason for Hezekiah's success was that he had cut down the idols and high places and the altars throughout Judah and even into Israel. This brings us to the record in II Chronicles 31. After the repentance at the feast and the removal of the idols, Hezekiah **"ordered the people living in Jerusalem to give the portion due the priests and Levites so they could devote themselves to the law of the Lord" (verse 4).** The people gave very generously of tithes and firstfruits and soon there was so much that the dedicated things were piled in heaps!

Here is where the second part of the principles that we are looking at in this chapter fits in. Not only did Hezekiah seek the Lord with all his heart and cause the people to do likewise, but also when what was given came in to the temple, he administered the gifts with wisdom. He set up a system of distribution. First he prepared storerooms in the temple and after this was done, the contributions were faithfully brought in and counted. Then Hezekiah set a Levite, Conaniah, in charge of the storehouse with his brother Shimei. Then Hezekiah appointed ten other men under these two to be in charge of the distribution. He also set up a process and other men in charge of what would be distributed to the various Levites and priests. Not one of the various Levites and priests was missed in the distribution.

We see several points here from what Hezekiah did NOT do: 1) Hezekiah did not keep all of the money in the temple "for a rainy day." He did not try to manipulate the control of the money in any way, 2) he did not set the high priest over the gifts, so that he would not be tempted to favor only certain priests, and 3) he did not have only a few to be in charge of the distribution. There were enough men involved in the determination of where the abundance went, so that there was a fair distribution.

These principles apply to us in a two-fold way. First, the care in administering gifts to the body of Christ is primarily the individual's responsibility. This goes along with so many of the other principles that we have studied. We need to seek God with all our heart and not count on our own resources. We need to also give the best gifts and not to cheat God in any way. But then, secondly, as stewards of the gifts given by other believers, pastors, church members, and leaders of various organizations all need to take heed to the example of Hezekiah for how to administer the gifts presented to them.

> **II Chronicles 31:20,21 (NIV):**
> **This is what Hezekiah did throughout Judah, doing what was good and right and faithful before the Lord his God.**
> **In everything that he undertook in the service of God's temple and in obedience to the law and the commands, he sought his God and worked wholeheartedly. And so he prospered.**

Hezekiah's prosperity and success in all his other endeavors, I believe, is directly related to how he was faithful regarding the stewardship of the service of God's temple. Part of seeking his God and working wholeheartedly had to do with enabling the Levites and priests to perform their functions in leading the worship of all Judah. Then Hezekiah himself also became very rich in material things.

In summation, true prosperity for Hezekiah came because his heart was set to seek after the Lord and then he was enabled to accomplish all that he intended and he faithfully administered the gifts for the needs of the temple. This helps to clarify a verse in the New Testament, which is very familiar to most Christians, II John 2. The Aramaic word for prosper is related to *tzaleack*.

II John 2 (Aramaic translation):
Our beloved, in everything I pray for you that you would prosper and be whole, even as your soul prospers.

Your soul prospers (accomplishes satisfactorily what is intended) as your heart seeks not the riches of the world, but the true riches of God. Then you will be able to accomplish great works and be successful in all that you do.

Study Questions

1) Are there any areas of your heart where you are not seeking God? Are you relying on your own ability in any way?
2) How was Hezekiah responsible for organizing the distribution of the gifts to the temple? How did he know what to do?
3) What other examples can you think of which have to do with being faithful in administering giving?

Chapter 7
Bountiful Blessings

No study on the topic of Biblical lessons on giving would be complete without searching Psalms and Proverbs for the wisdom contained there. We have laid out this chapter in subtopics, with a representation of verses included from several translations, so that the truth of the Word can speak for itself. You can personalize these verses and add more to them to use for memorization, and much contemplation. Then the study questions include many other words that can be investigated.

No Lack

One of the most wonderful promises for those who apply the principles we have been studying is that they will have no lack. By looking at the opposite first, we will see again that all the provision comes from God.

Psalm 34:9, 10 (Lamsa):
The rich have become poor and suffer hunger;
They that seek the Lord shall not lack any good thing.

Psalm 37:18, 19 and 25 (NIV):
The days of the blameless are known to the Lord, and their inheritance will endure forever.
In times of disaster they will not wither; in days of famine they will enjoy plenty.

I was young and now I am old, yet I have never seen the righteous forsaken or their children begging bread.

Proverbs 10:3 (Lamsa):
The Lord will not suffer the soul of the righteous to famish; but he casts away the substance of the wicked.

Riches and Honor

Riches and honor are the result of reverence of the Lord and applying wisdom as discussed in Proverbs.

Proverbs 3:16, 17 (CEV):
In her right hand
    Wisdom holds a long life,
And in her left hand
    Are wealth and honor.
Wisdom makes life pleasant
    And leads us safely along.
Wisdom is a life-giving tree,
The source of happiness
    For all who hold on to her.

Proverbs 8:18, 35 (KJV):
Riches and honour are with me [wisdom]; *yea*, durable riches and righteousness.
For whoso findeth me findeth life, and shall obtain favour of the Lord.

Proverbs 10:4 (Lamsa):
Poverty humbles a man; but the hands of diligent men make rich.

Proverbs 22:4 (NIV):
Humility and the fear of the Lord bring wealth and honor and life.

Plenty

Being filled or satisfied with plenty is the result of seeking God first and obeying His precepts.

Job 22:21 (Moffatt):
Give way to God, submit to him, and it will mean prosperity for you;

Psalm 22:26 (Darby):
The meek shall eat and be satisfied; they shall praise Jehovah that seek him: your heart shall live forever.

Psalm 147:11, 14 (NIV):
The Lord delights in those who fear him, who put their hope in his unfailing love.
He grants peace to your borders and satisfies you with the finest of wheat.

Proverbs 3:9, 10 (KJV):
Honour the Lord with thy substance, and with the firstfruits of all thine increase:
So shall thy barns be filled with plenty, and thy presses shall burst out with new wine.

Proverbs 8:21 (KJV):
That I [wisdom] may cause those that love me to inherit substance; and I will fill their treasures.

Malachi 3:10 (NIV):
Bring the whole tithe into the storehouse, that there may be food in my house. Test me in this," says the Lord Almighty, "and see if I will not throw open the floodgates of heaven and pour out so much blessing that you will not have room enough for it.

Long Life and Health

A long life and health to enjoy it are certainly two of the greatest blessings that God bestows on the righteous.

Psalm 103:3-5 (CEV):
The Lord forgives our sins,
heals us when we are sick
    and protects us from death.
His kindness and love
    are a crown on our heads.
Each day that we live,
    he provides for our needs
and gives us the strength
    of a young eagle.

Psalm 91:15, 16 (KJV):
He shall call upon me, and I will answer him: I *will be* **with him in trouble; I will deliver him, and honour him.**
With long life will I satisfy him, and show him my salvation.

Proverbs 3:1, 2, 7, 8 (NIV):
My Son, do not forget my teaching, but keep my commands in your heart,

For they will prolong your life many years and bring you prosperity.
Do not be wise in your own eyes; fear the Lord and shun evil.
This will bring health to your body and nourishment to your bones.

Proverbs 4:20, 22 (KJV):
My son, attend to my words; incline thine ear unto my sayings.
For they *are* life unto those that find them, and health to all their flesh.

Proverbs 9:11 (NIV):
For through me [the fear of the Lord] your days will be many, and years will be added to your life.

The next three subtopics are filled with nuggets of wisdom for those who have "ears to hear."

Give Generously

Generosity emphasizes the WAY that we give. We could give grudgingly, feeling that we have to, but the results are not the same as when giving with generosity, freely. I have chosen to quote the verses in this subtopic from the New International Version, because it translates the Hebrew word as "generous."

Psalm 37:21, 26 (NIV):
The wicked borrow and do not repay, but the righteous give generously.
They are always generous and lend freely; their children will be blessed.

Psalm 112:5 (NIV):
Good will come to him who is generous and lends freely, who conducts his affairs with justice.

Proverbs 11:25 (NIV):
A generous man will prosper; he who refreshes others will himself be refreshed.

Proverbs 22:9 (NIV):
A generous man will himself be blessed, for he shares his food with the poor.

Don't Be Lazy

The word "lazy" is not in the King James Version. The words to study are "slothful" or "sluggard." As it is used in the Bible, being lazy means not only to avoid work and business, but also to chase fantasies. This confronts all "get rich quick" schemes that are so prevalent in our day and time.

Proverbs 6:6-8 (KJV):
Go to the ant, thou sluggard; consider her ways, and be wise;
Which having no guide, overseer, or ruler,
Provideth her meat in the summer, *and* gathereth her food in the harvest.

Proverbs 12:24 (CEV):
Word hard, and you
**   will be a leader;**
Be lazy, and you
**   will end up a slave.**

Proverbs 19:15 (KJV):
Slothfulness casteth into a deep sleep; and an idle soul shall suffer hunger.

Proverbs 20:13 (NIV):
Do not love sleep or you will grow poor; stay awake and you will have food to spare.

Proverbs 24:30-34 (Lamsa):
I passed by the field of a sluggard, and by the vineyard of the man void of understanding,
And, lo, it was all grown over with thorns, and nettles had covered the face thereof, and its stone wall was broken down.
Then I looked upon it, and considered it well, and I received instruction:
Yet a little sleep, a little slumber, a little folding of the hands upon your chest;
So shall poverty come upon you, and want shall overtake you suddenly like a runner.

Proverbs 28:19, 20 (NIV):
He who works his land will have abundant food, but the one who chases fantasies will have his fill of poverty.
A faithful man will be richly blessed, but one eager to get rich will not go unpunished.

Don't Trust in Wealth

The last subtopic pertains to not trusting in riches or wealth. The opposite would be to trust in the provision of God. (Remember the manna?)

Ecclesiastes 5:10 (NIV):
Whoever loves money never has money enough;
whoever loves wealth is never satisfied with his
income. This too is meaningless.

Psalm 52:7 (KJV):
Lo, *this is* the man *that* made not God his strength;
but trusted in the abundance of his riches, *and*
strengthened himself in his wickedness.

Psalm 62:10 (KJV):
Trust not in oppression, and become not vain in
robbery: if riches increase, set not your heart
upon them.

Proverbs 11:28 (Moffatt):
He who relies on his wealth shall wither, but a
good man blooms like a green leaf.

Proverbs 23:4, 5 (NIV):
Do not wear yourself out to get rich; have the
wisdom to show restraint.
Cast but a glance at riches, and they are gone, for
they will surely sprout wings and fly off to the sky
like an eagle.

Proverbs 30:8 (NIV):
Keep falsehood and lies far from me; give me
neither poverty nor riches, but give me only my
daily bread.

There is a wonderful verse that summarizes the gladness
of heart that comes from practicing each of these principles.
We may have the blessings of long life, health, plenty, even
riches and honor, but without being happy in our work, these

blessings are not appreciated. This truly is the most bountiful gift from God.

> **Ecclesiastes 5:18-20 (NIV):**
> **Then I realized that it is good and proper for a man to eat and drink, and to find satisfaction in his toilsome labor under the sun during the few days of life God has given him—for this is his lot.**
> **Moreover, when God gives any man wealth and possessions, and enables him to enjoy them, to accept his lot and be happy in his word—this is a gift of God.**
> **He seldom reflects on the days of his life, because God keeps him occupied with gladness of heart.**

Study Questions

Below are words to study in this context of bountiful blessings:

1) bounty, bountiful
2) wealth
3) fat, fertile
4) abundant, abundance
5) possessions
6) satisfied, satisfaction
7) overflowing, much
8) prosper, success

Chapter 8
Alms for the Poor

Passage to Study: Deuteronomy 24:10-22; Matthew 6:1-4

Most people's reactions to being confronted with a group of beggars is to try to ignore them as much as possible. In fact, to ignore the poor is the general mandate of our culture. We figure that welfare and other charitable programs are taking care of the problem. Jesus said, **"the poor you will always have with you."** We take the verse out of context and use it as an excuse not to do anything about it (Matthew 26:11). This lesson will answer three questions that will make us more aware of the need for giving alms: 1) Who are the poor? 2) What should we give to the poor? 3) How should we give to the poor?

Who are the poor?

In Deuteronomy 14, we saw that every three years the tithe was to stay in the locality of the Levites and be given to the poor. There are four categories of people who are described in these verses who are the poor.

Deuteronomy 14:28, 29 (NIV):
At the end of every three years, bring all the tithes of that year's produce and store it in your town,
So that the Levites (who have no allotment or inheritance of their own) and the aliens, the fatherless and the widows who live in your towns may come and eat and be satisfied, and so that the Lord your God may bless you in all the work of your hands.

ENRICHED IN EVERYTHING

The four categories are: 1) Levites, 2) aliens, 3) fatherless, and 4) widows. The reasons to give to the Levites were discussed in chapter 4 and 5. It is very interesting that the Levites are considered among the poor.

Aliens are the strangers or foreigners who dwell with the families in the towns. They may be Gentiles or they may be travelers who are far from their homes. The Hebrew word is *ger* and often is translated "sojourner." In our vernacular, it would relate to people who are from another location who move in to our city or community. They desire to dwell there, but often because of language differences, education, and background, it is difficult for them to get jobs.

The difference between a "sojourner" and a "citizen" in the Old Testament is related to whether or not they own property. Someone who has established themselves in a community and is enjoying the rights of the citizens is no longer considered an alien. Ruth is an example of someone in this category. She came to the land of Israel with Naomi, and was considered a "stranger" until she married Boaz.

The reason that this category of people is very special to God's heart is that Israel was often in this situation of dwelling in a foreign land. Other nations oppressed Israel even to the point of slavery. But God says that they should do the opposite. The hospitality customs in the East originated from this portion of the Law. Every traveler who came into a town would be taken care of with food and lodging. No one was allowed to sleep in the streets without a place to stay.

The word "homeless" has a rather negative connotation in our society, but that is truly what is meant by alien. Anyone can be homeless for a period of time. Perhaps they are traveling, or moving to a new city, or coming in to a country as an immigrant, or even just searching for a new job in a community. The point is that this category of people should be taken care of, and particularly not oppressed in any way.

The third category of people who are poor are those who are "fatherless." This means orphans or those who do not

59

have a family to support them. There is a beautiful verse, Psalm 68:5, where God says that he is **"a father of the fatherless, and a judge of the widows...God setteth the solitary in families."** We are to especially guard against taking advantage of children who are fatherless as in Proverbs 23:10: **"Do not move an ancient boundary stone, or encroach on the fields of the fatherless, for their Defender is strong; he will take up their case against you."** I believe that this applies to those who are alone in any category, not only children with no parents. The root verb in Hebrew for orphan means to be lonely. There are many lonely people today whose families do not take care of them. It can also apply to situations where there are disasters such as earthquakes, fires, or floods, when one's home and possessions are destroyed for a time and people find themselves alone.

The fourth category of people who are poor are those who are widows. A widow is one who does not have a husband. In the strict use of the word, this is a woman whose husband has died and who has no children to support her. However, we can extend the application in the New Testament church to single men and women, especially those who are caring for young ones. I am reminded of the love Jesus had for the widow who gave the two small mites in the Temple. I Timothy 5 gives specific advice about how to determine who is really a widow. The charge is to families to care for their own widows, so that the church may support those who are truly widows in need. **"Give proper recognition to those widows who are really in need."**

These four categories of people described in Deuteronomy 24 are those **"who are within your gates."** It is not possible to care for all the poor in every place, so we are to be concerned about those who live in our communities first. If everyone applied this, there would be no need for programs such as welfare and national distributions to endeavor to meet this need.

The New Testament describes two other groups of people who are poor. The first is the sick and those who are tormented by evil spirits. The record of the man at the temple gate Beautiful was laid at the gate and asked alms of those that entered into the temple, not because he was so poor financially, but because he had a great need. Most often, when someone is sick, they are not able to work and to earn a living. Whatever savings they have gets consumed with the expenses of being sick also. As Peter and John passed by the man at the gate, Peter said to him: **"Silver and gold have I none, but what I have I give you. In the name of Jesus Christ of Nazareth, walk."** What is needed by these people in this category is not necessarily money, but healing.

The second group was already mentioned briefly in regard to orphans. Any disaster such as would cause famine, fire, floods, etc. is a specific time when we should be concerned with those who are from other places. II Corinthians 8 discusses a time when there was a famine in Jerusalem and Paul sent Titus with a special offering to care for the people who were in Jerusalem. It does not specifically say that they gave only to the believers, but there was a special concern that the people in the church were taken care of. In Acts 24:17, Paul goes to Jerusalem, and he is bringing **"alms to my nation."** The famine lasted a long time in that area, and people were under severe hardship.

To summarize, we have categories of people who are considered to be poor, even if they are not poor for an extended period of time: Levites (or ministers), the homeless, orphans and widows, those suffering from sickness or disaster. It is God's special encouragement that these people be helped with whatever their need is, and this is to whom we are to give alms or charity.

ALMS FOR THE POOR

What should we give to the poor?

Deuteronomy 14 sets the precedent for what should be given to the poor.

Deuteronomy 14:19-22 (Lamsa):
When you reap the harvest in your field, and have forgotten a sheaf in the field, you shall not return to fetch it; it shall be for the stranger, for the fatherless, and for the widow, that the Lord your God may bless you in all the works of your hands.
When you beat your olive trees, you shall not go over the boughs again; it shall be for the stranger, for the orphan, and for the widow.
When you gather the grapes of your vineyard, you shall not glean it afterward; it shall be for the stranger, for the fatherless, and for the widow.
And you shall remember that you were a bondman in Egypt; therefore I command you to do this thing.

The Law set up a way for the poor to be able to have provision in gleaning from the fields. Read the record of Ruth again and see the beautiful example of how she went to the fields to gather the leftover harvest from the barley fields. Even though in our culture we do not generally have fields whereby we can leave some of the harvest, we do work for companies where there is much excess that is just thrown away. This extra (whether it be computers, supplies, clothes, food) is what should be left for the poor. Every grocery store used to have a place where you could go to get day old bread and overripe fruits and vegetables. What happened to this idea? It also used to be that after a harvest, anyone could go to the fields and pick "drop apples" or leftover tomatoes, etc. It is now a crime to go into anyone else's property to "glean" the fields, even when the food is sitting and rotting away. We are too afraid today of having lawsuits, so that this practice has been neglected.

In Acts 7 of the New Testament, the early Church had set up a system of distribution to the poor and needy and this is an example to us today also. Seven men with the Spirit of God were set up as "deacons" to oversee the distribution of food and other necessities. Instead of having rummage sales at our churches, there should be stations where plurality of possessions can be brought and distributed to "those in our gates" who need them. It takes men and women **who are full of the Spirit of the Lord and of wisdom"** to be appointed to this task. Otherwise, there is much temptation to play favorites in the distribution and to end up being hypocrites with this type of giving.

Since today we do not have the Law as in the Old Testament and the principle of gleaning, the care of the poor resides with the love that the Church has for ALL its members, as well as the community. In this, we show the love our Father has for his children and we make known our loving Father to those in our community not yet introduced to him. Too often, we, as a body in general, selfishly hold plurality to ourselves, and do not distribute it. Oh that the testimony of the early Church would again be ours:

Acts 4:32, 34, 35 (ISV):
Now the whole group of believers was one in heart and soul, and nobody called any of his possessions his own. Instead, they shared everything they owned.
For none of them needed anything, because all who had land or houses would sell them and bring the money received for the things sold and lay it at the apostles' feet.
Then it was distributed to anyone who needed it.

ALMS FOR THE POOR

How do we give to the poor?

Matthew 6:1-4 details the method by which we should give alms. Just as when we pray, it should be in our own closet, so when we give charity, it should not be seen.

Matthew 6:1-4 (NIV):
"Be careful not to do your 'acts of righteousness' before men, to be seen by them. If you do, you will have no reward from your Father in heaven.
So when you give to the needy, do not announce it with trumpets, as the hypocrites do in the synagogues and on the streets, to be honored by men. I tell you the truth, they have received their reward in full.
But when you give to the needy, do not let your left hand know what your right hand is doing,
So that your giving may be in secret. Then your Father, who sees what is done in secret, will reward you.

It is impossible to have your left hand not know what your right hand is doing. Likewise, it is not always possible for someone to know where a gift came from. But we do not need to broadcast the fact that we gave to the poor, by requesting our names to be on a donation, by making public proclamations of the charity, or even by asking for receipts and acknowledgements. Insomuch as it is possible, make any giving of this type anonymously and in secret. That way the thanksgiving by the recipient can go to God and God will take care of the blessing to you. Otherwise it is too easy to want to be honored by men for our "generosity." Who is the one in your community that God has put on your heart to help in time of need? If your church or fellowship does not have a station of distribution, how can you help to set one up?

ENRICHED IN EVERYTHING

Most of the time, alms should take the form of actual food, clothing, or necessities. Giving money to poor does not usually have good results. What people in need want is for someone to help them to get out of that position. If someone is sick, they need healing. If someone has had a catastrophe in their life, they need provision for the moment. If someone needs a job, they need encouragement and help with ideas from those around, in order to secure one. Perhaps they need help with learning skills to qualify for a job, or time to take special education. Perhaps a widow or single woman with children needs help with after school care, so that they do not have to pay an exorbitant rate for childcare. Perhaps someone lives alone and is not able to drive or travel by himself to get groceries. Perhaps there is a minister who has need for a different car, so that he may continue to minister to his congregation. The reason it is necessary to have people in whom the Spirit of God is to oversee the distribution is that the poor are the cases that are usually missed. When someone has a need, it is very difficult to have to request special help. Most of the time, it is far easier to live with the situation, than to make the need known. Let us become aware of the needs of our fellow believers and of those in the community, and begin to set up methods whereby these needs can be met!

Study Questions

1) Make a list and title the four categories of "poor." Then write the names of the people that you know of in each category. Then determine what you can specifically do to help each one.
2) Consider what the criteria are for "widows indeed" using the passage in I Timothy.
3) What types of organizations to help the poor are effective and which are not? Why?

4) Find out about programs in your community that are helping people in these categories. How can you participate in any way?
5) Why are the Levites classed among the poor? Is this still true today that ministers are "poor"? How and in what way?

Chapter 9
The Simple Life

What is the simple life? It is described in Matthew 6 in the Sermon on the Mount.

Matthew 6:22-24 (KJV):
The light of the body is the eye: if therefore thine eye be single, thy whole body shall be full of light. But if thine eye be evil, thy whole body shall be full of darkness. If therefore the light that is in thee be darkness, how great *is* that darkness! No man can serve two masters: for either he will hate the one, and love the other; or else he will hold to the one, and despise the other. Ye cannot serve God and mammon.

There are a number of different translations of verse 22 that try to make sense of it to us in our culture: "if your eyesight is good," "if your eye is sound." The commentaries try to explain what this means. If we understand the Hebrew idiom in this phrase, then the whole passage fits in context and the reason for the conclusion, "you cannot serve God and mammon," is made clear.

First of all, the word "light" in the King James means lamp in Aramaic. The eye is the place of reflection of the inner part of one's being. The true feelings and will of a person shine out of the eyes. This phrase is a metaphor, emphasizing that the eye is like a lamp. The comparison is used to relate the familiar aspects of a lamp with what shines out of a man's heart. This is fully explained and developed in the synoptic passage in Luke 11:34-36. Verse 36 clarifies the metaphor: "**If**

67

thy whole body therefore *be* full of light, having no part dark, the whole shall be full of light, as when the bright shining of a candle doth give thee light." When what is inside you is dark, there will not be much light shining out, but when your whole being is light, it will shine as a bright candle does. This now sets the stage for the point of the passage.

The idiom, "if your eye is single," means "to be generous." To be evil is to be greedy or stingy. [8] The Aramaic word for single in this passage is *peshita*, which is the name for the whole New Testament text that we are studying. *Peshita* means simple or straight. There are many other passages that are now clarified when we understand that the Aramaic and Hebrew idea of being "simple" means to be generous. Here are just a few examples:

II Corinthians 8:2 (KJV):
How that in a great trial of affliction the abundance of their joy and their deep poverty abounded unto the riches of their liberality. [The word liberality is simplicity in Aramaic.]

Colossians 3:22 (KJV):
Servants, obey in all things *your* masters according to the flesh; not with eyeservice, as menpleasers; but in singleness of heart, fearing God:
And whatsoever ye do, do *it* heartily, as to the Lord, and not unto men; [Singleness of heart is "with a simple heart" in Aramaic.]

---

[8] Bivin, David and Blizzard, Roy, *Understanding the Difficult Words of Jesus*, p.144-145.

Romans 12:8 (KJV):
Or he that exhorteth, on exhortation: he that giveth, *let him do it* **with simplicity**...[Simplicity is *peshita.*]

James 1:5 (KJV):
Now if any of you lack wisdom, let him ask of God, that giveth to all *men* **liberally, and upbraideth not; and it shall be given him.** [Here the idiom for simplicity is translated in its meaning, rather than literally.]

The opposite "evil eye" refers to being miserly or selfish. [9] Proverbs 28:22 says, **"He who hastens to be rich has an evil eye and considers not that poverty shall come upon him"** [Lamsa]. A person who is greedy and selfish will continually take from others and use them.   He may get rich in the process, but ultimately, poverty will be his reward. This is emphasized in the passage in Luke 11. **"Take heed therefore that the light which is in thee be not darkness."**

The conclusion of this passage is that **"you cannot serve God and mammon."**   Mammon is a Chaldean word that means literally "that in which one trusts," hence wealth or riches. [10] The argument of this passage is based on one of the seven rules of Hillel. This was a school of rabbis during the time of Jesus Christ headed by Hillel, who set forth rules to follow when interpreting or understanding the scriptures. These were known for many years and passed down among the priests, but Hillel was the first one to write them down. The first rule is called *kal v'khomer* and means "light and heavy." It may be expressed as follows: if X is true of Y, then how much

---

[9] Gaebelein, Frank E., *The Expositor's Bible Commentary*, Volume 8, p.178.
[10] Bullinger, E.W., *A Critical Lexicon and Concordance to the English and Greek New Testament,* p. 476.

more X must be true of Z. [11] It is applied in this passage to bring weight to the idea of serving riches. If you are generous, your life is full of light. If you are stingy and greedy, your life is full of darkness. How great is that darkness when you SERVE wealth as a lord! The play on words where light and darkness represents God and mammon is also very revealing.

What is the lesson? Be generous and your whole life will be simple and straightforward and full of light! We can translate the Aramaic: **"The lamp of the body is the eye. Therefore if you are generous, your whole body is enlightened."**

Study Questions

1) Are there any places in your life where you are not being generous? How can they be changed?
2) Explain how the eye is the lamp of the body.
3) What are some other examples of the metaphors of light and darkness?
4) What is mammon? What does it mean to you?
5) How can you simplify your own life? List some examples.

[11] Trimm, James, *Seven Rules of Hillel*, p. 1-2.

Chapter 10
Pressed Down, Shaken Together and Running Over

Passage to Study: Luke 6:17-49

This chapter has to do with our business in the context of giving and presents some "do's and don'ts." Luke 6:17-49 is known as the teaching "on the plain." It is similar to the Sermon on the Mount and is also given near the Sea of Galilee. It includes some of the same "Beatitudes" as Matthew 6, but the blessings are contrasted by "woes."

There are four lessons in this section of Luke. We will see that these are woven together with "light and heavy" teaching, a typical teaching method of the rabbis. The lessons are:

1. Don't choose present gratification over future blessing, but give to everyone.
2. Don't just "give to get," but give with mercy; give even when you don't get anything back.
3. Don't laugh at the expense of others and judge selfishly, but give good measure, forgive and respect others.
4. Don't speak falsely and seek men's praise, but give from the heart with integrity.

There are four "woes" that set the opposite context for the lessons in the sermon.

Luke 6:24-26 (Aramaic translation):
But woe to you, rich [ones], because you have received your comfort!

71

PRESSED DOWN, SHAKEN TOGETHER AND RUNNING OVER

Woe to you, satisfied [ones], because you will hunger! Woe to you who are laughing now, because you will cry and you will mourn!
Woe to you, when men will speak what is good about you, for their fathers did likewise to the false prophets!

Woe to the rich

The first woe is regarding those who are rich: **"Woe to you rich ones, for you have received your comfort!"** The opposite is, "blessed are the poor." It is using the idea of physical riches and poverty to explain the first lesson above: don't choose present gratification over future blessing, but give to everyone. "Blessed are the poor" does not mean that material poverty is a great way to live. But it is referring to those who count on physical riches and rely upon those, instead of God. Wealth often predisposes men to think they have need of nothing. That kind of prosperity yields a comfort in the physical life, but often an inner emptiness. Are you reminded of some of our first lessons in giving from the Old Testament? We are to stop relying on our own ability to get wealth and instead, to give to everyone.

The solutions for how to stop depending on riches are in verses 27-28:

Luke 6:27-28 (Aramaic translation):
But to you who hear, I say, 'Love your enemies and do that which is good to those who harm you. Bless those who malign you and pray for those who take you by force.

These solutions all have to do with giving. Give to everyone! Don't choose who you wish to help based on whether they are friend or enemy. Most people who are rich only help those who cater to them or who can help them with further gain. And if you get on the "bad side" of someone who is wealthy, it usually means that there will be repercussions from them. What is normally taught with this verse is to "turn the other cheek." This section is specifically talking to those who are wealthy to give without discrimination and to use that kind of giving to maintain reliance on God first, not their wealth. Give to everyone, even those who hurt you (remember also to pray for them).

Woe to the satisfied ones

The second woe is to "satisfied [ones]" and illustrates the lesson of being merciful. Those who are satisfied think they know how to get wealth and tend to be smug in that knowledge. The world's way of getting wealth is "giving to get." You only give if you will get something in return. Mercy is a deliberate pouring out of kindness or love, often in spite of what is deserved. The lesson is to do more than just not "giving to get," but give with mercy, give even when you don't get anything back.

This mercy extends to very specific circumstances. What to do instead of "giving to get" is spelled out in verses 29-31.

Luke 6:29-31 (Aramaic translation):
And to him, who strikes you on your cheek, offer to him the other, and from him, who takes away your outer cloak, do not hold back your tunic also. To everyone who asks you, give to him, and from him, who takes away your property, do not demand [it] back.
And whatever you desire men to do to you, you do the same to them also.

PRESSED DOWN, SHAKEN TOGETHER AND RUNNING OVER

There is a figure of speech in this section. It is called *anaphora* or "like beginnings" and the repetition is set in an alternation. Here is a chart to describe the figure:

A.	And to him …offer
B	And from him …do not hold back
A	And to him …give
B	And from him…do not demand it back

The emphasis of this figure of speech is on the words that are repeated. In this case, how to deal with someone if you are in these circumstances is what is emphasized: "to" and "from." Don't hold back, don't demand something in return – GIVE to everyone, even someone who does something wrong to you.

To him who strikes you on your cheek refers to someone who insults you or shames you in some category. In the East, if you slap someone on the cheek, it is a very great insult. All of these circumstances: insults, taking away your cloak, borrowing, taking away something that you own, are not very positive situations. The point is that despite something specific being taken from you, GIVE instead. The conclusion of the section is in verse 31: **"And whatever you want men to do to you, you do the same to them also."** If you want others to give to you, in spite of the fact that sometimes you do not deserve it, then give even in negative circumstances.

This theme continues in verses 32-36:

Luke 6:32-34 (Aramaic translation):
For if you love those who love you, what is your grace? For even sinners love those who love them. And if you do that which is good to those who do well to you, what is your grace? For even sinners do the same.

74

And if you lend to [those from] whom you expect to be repaid, what is your goodness? For even sinners lend to sinners that in the same way they might be repaid.

This section has two figures of speech: 1) *erotesis*, or questioning, and 2) *anadiplosis*, like endings. The question is designed to be thought provoking and not necessarily to be answered directly. There is a question that is repeated three times as an ending: **"What is your goodness?"** Goodness means favor in giving. If you only give to those who give to you, what is your giving? Remember, this section is to the "satisfied ones." If you only give to those who give to you, that is not mercy. Mercy is giving in spite of what is deserved. Even sinners give when others give to them. But the true satisfaction comes from giving in spite of circumstances. The conclusion is in verse 35 and 36: **"do not give up hope of anyone, and your reward will be increased and you will be the sons of the Most High, because he is kind to the evil and to the unthankful. Therefore be merciful, as your Father also is merciful."**

Woe to those who laugh

The next part of the lesson is: don't laugh at the expense of others and judge selfishly, but give good measure, forgive and respect others. There are four commands in verses 37-38:

Luke 6:37-38 (Aramaic translation):
Do not judge and you will not be judged. Do not condemn and you will not be condemned. Forgive and you will be forgiven.
Give and it will be given to you, with good and pressed down and abundant measure they will throw into your lap. For with the same measure you measure, it will be measured to you."

PRESSED DOWN, SHAKEN TOGETHER AND RUNNING OVER

This woe pertains to the measure that you measure. The commands are: do not judge, do not condemn, forgive, and give. One could say this in a different way: "what you give out is what you get back." If you give out judgment (in the sense of pronouncing someone guilty), you will get judgment. If you give out condemnation, you will get condemnation. If you give out forgiveness, you will get forgiveness back. If you give, it will be given to you. Thus how MUCH you give and HOW you give will be measured back to you.

The phrase about "good and pressed down and abundant measure" is related to the Oriental custom of measuring grain at the market. There was actually a special person who was known as the measurer. He was an impartial person, not the buyer or seller, and he would measure out the grain into a *timneh*, or measuring basket. Then he would shake it, press it down, and pour in more until it was overflowing. This was done several times in order to give a "good measure." Then the measure was poured into the large pocket (or bosom) of the buyer's cloak. There was a difference of almost 30% added to the total measure by filling the basket in this fashion. [12]

Verses 39-44 contain three examples that are the "light teaching" for this third point. They are all connected with "woe to those who laugh" but are emphasizing the specific points already taught.

1. Blind leading the blind (vs. 39-40)
    *   Everyone who is mature will follow the example of the master in not condemning or laughing at others who have not.

2. Straw and plank (vs. 41-42)
    *   See what faults God has forgiven you for before you condemn others

---

[12] Neil, *Palestine Explored*, p. 34.

3. Good and bad trees (vs. 43-45)
    *   We are known by our fruit. What we say shows what is
        in our heart.

Woe to false speaking

The last lesson in Luke 6 is to beware of men when they
speak good things about you that are false. Praise undeserved
is the worst kind of flattery. Don't speak falsely and seek
men's praise. The antidote is to give from the heart with
integrity. "Practice what you preach."

> **Luke 6:45-49 (Aramaic translation):**
> **Why do you call me, 'My Lord, my Lord,' and
> you do not do what I say?**
> **I will show you what each one who comes to me
> and hears my words and does them is like.**
> **He is like the man who built a house and dug and
> went deep and laid the foundations upon rock.
> And when there was a flood, the flood beat on that
> house, and it was not able to shake it, for its
> foundation was placed upon rock.**
> **And whoever hears [my words] and does not do
> [them] is like the man who built his house upon
> ground without a foundation. And when the river
> beat upon it, immediately it fell, and the fall of
> that house was great."**

If we call on Jesus as Lord and praise him, but do not do what
he says, that is this kind of flattery and false speaking. We seek
praise from men for our religious show, but there is no
foundation of truly making Jesus Lord in our lives. We are like
a man who builds a house without a foundation. When the
storms of attack from Satan come, the house falls, because it

was not built on anything solid. That which is solid is the truth of God's word and the truth being spoken on our lips, backed up by true actions.

An example from our culture may help here. Most of us do not build our own houses, so we have trouble relating to this illustration. However, almost all of us have employers in some form or another. For example, I say to my employer, "I think you are the greatest boss! I am so happy to work for you!" Then I turn around and speak critical words to my co-workers about him behind his back like, "He never gets his act together. Who does he think he is anyway? I could do his job too!" And then I refuse to follow my employer's direction about a task, because I think that I know better. I put this in the first person, because I have been tempted to do these very things in specific categories many times. Have you ever experienced this?

But if I cheerfully give my heart and time and endeavor to follow my employer's directions, then when I say, "Thank you for all you do for me," it rings true. My actions show the integrity of my giving. I will receive deserved praise rather than false speaking in return.

These four "woes" have much food for thought in them and this chapter in Luke is rich with many lessons that one could preach on for a month! But in regard to giving, there are specific "do's" when we change the negative to positive: give to everyone, give with mercy, give good measure, and give with integrity.

Study Questions

1) Think about any times when you have not given to someone because they had hurt you. What could you do instead?

2) What is your motivation when you give to your church or any other organization? What should be the kind of attitude we have, for example, regarding mission work?

3) Are there any planks to take out of your own eye before you can see clearly? What measure are you giving out in terms of judgment?

4) Is there an area of your Christian life where you are not practicing the words of our Lord? Start building the foundation for the house.

5) Is there need for repentance regarding speaking false flattery?

Chapter 11
Freely - Without A Cause

A believer's justification is totally God's gift of grace. It is neither deserved nor merited, but it is given because God loved us. We saw this in the introduction regarding God's motivation for giving.

John 3:16 (KJV):
For God so loved the world, that he gave his only begotten Son, that whosoever believeth in him should not perish, but have everlasting life.

God gave His only begotten son so that we could have eternal life. This kind of giving is the ultimate example of what we should be giving. This can be seen and understood vividly by a study of the words that are translated "freely."

One of the words for freely, *dorean*, literally means "without a cause." It can also be translated gratuitously, as a gift, out of favor, for no reason, unnecessarily. It is used in Romans 3:24 to show how God justified us.

Romans 3:24 (KJV):
Being justified freely by his grace through the redemption that is in Christ Jesus:

God justified us, acquitted us from guilt, without a cause. He did not have a reason for doing this other than His grace. There was nothing that we did to deserve the justification. We did not earn it. It was "out of favor," "as a gift." A gift is the antithesis of wages. Thus receiving the gift of justification and righteousness is "gratuitous," determined by God's goodness and love, not by our works, good, or bad.

If God did this kind of giving, don't you think that we should **"be imitators of God, therefore, as dearly loved children"** (Ephesians 5:1) and copy his attitude? If someone does not **deserve** our giving, isn't it any more reason to do something for him or her? Does someone have to deserve our favor, before we give it? This is especially true in light of ministering the gospel to people, Christians or not. We received God's favor without deserving it, didn't we?

Another way to translate *dorean* is without cost or expense. Salvation is without cost to us who receive it by faith, but it cost God the death of his only begotten Son! Matthew 10:8, **"freely you have received, freely give,"** is an exhortation by Jesus to his disciples when he sent them out to heal the sick and preach the word. In essence, he was saying that they had received the word freely, without cost, and should now go and give that to others. Freely giving means to preach the gospel of the good news of our salvation and righteousness. Making the gospel without cost to others is the way that Paul preached.

II Corinthians 11:7 (ISV):
Did I commit a sin when I humbled myself by proclaiming to you the gospel of God free of charge, so that you could be exalted?

In Jesus Christ we are justified without a cause, as a gift. In Jesus Christ we received redemption and righteousness. In Jesus Christ we can reign in life. This is salvation and wholeness and includes our life now as well as eternal life. Should we not do the greatest giving and get busy sharing this good news?

Romans 8:32 (KJV):
He that spared not his own Son, but delivered him
up for us all, how shall he not with him also freely
give us all things?

The word for "freely give" in this verse is *charizomai*. Its root is from *charis*, grace. Our justification was not based on works, but grace. So also our life continues on that basis. Our reigning in life now is by God's grace and continued giving to us as His sons.

Titus 3:5-7 (KJV):
Not by works of righteousness which we have
done, but according to his mercy he saved us, by
the washing of regeneration, and renewing of the
Holy Ghost;
Which he shed on us abundantly through Jesus
Christ our Saviour;
That being justified by his grace, we should be
made heirs according to the hope of eternal life.

God saved us and abundantly poured out His acceptance out on us. He declared that we were accepted in the beloved, in Christ Jesus. This pouring out of His grace is clear in the Aramaic translation of Ephesians 1:6.

Ephesians 1:6 (Aramaic translation):
that the glory of his grace may be glorified, which
he poured forth upon us by the hand of his
beloved [one],

From this brief look at the words for freely, the magnificence of God's grace can be realized even more. Without a cause, freely, as a gift, God poured out His love and justified us, gave us righteousness, eternal life. He continues to freely give so that we can reign in life now. This is not based upon any merit or deserving, but is all by HIS LOVE. The gospel did not cost us anything, yet we can turn around and give it to others. We can preach the gospel "freely." What a privilege – to be an imitator of God and to allow others to drink from the fountain of life freely!

Revelation 21:6 (NIV):
To him who is thirsty I will give to drink without cost from the spring of the water of life.

Study Questions

1) Think of someone who does not "deserve" your giving and write down an example of something you can do for him or her.
2) What does *dorean* mean?
3) How does grace tie in with giving freely?
4) Write down someone you can think of to whom you could "freely give" the gospel today.

Chapter 12
The Grace of Giving

There are many discussions and disputes regarding the application of tithing to the New Testament church and the necessity of giving at least 10% of our income to the church. Many churches use this teaching to make sure that they have enough money to run the business of the church and periodically pull out the teaching about financial abundance mostly to boost the current budget. Leaving these disputes and the motivation of church budgets aside, what do the Church epistles say about giving and how can I as a believer determine what to give and how to give?

The issue is not between tithing and giving. The issue is that giving is something that God wants us to do. Most people who argue against the application of tithing in our day and time are not giving in any capacity and see this argument as a reason (or may I say excuse) not to give at all. I believe that of all the passages that speak about giving in the Church epistles particularly, II Corinthians 8 and 9 set the foundation for the practical application of giving for us today. These chapters set forth a cycle of the "grace of giving." In this chapter we will examine this cycle and see how it answers the questions posed above.

II Corinthians was written to the church in Corinth to reprove situations that had crept into the church in the practical side of their lives. This reproof is directed to the church as a whole and the situation that had happened in Corinth is the same that is in many churches today. The believers had made verbal statements that they wanted to give to help the outreach of the ministry to the saints, especially to Jerusalem, but they had not followed through with the action to do the actual giving. The passage does not deal with the

84

excuses or reasons that certainly were posed regarding why they had not followed through with the giving. It deals with the correct process of giving which needs to be in place and sets this forth so that the believers would understand why they should follow through on their original desire to help with the ministry of the saints.

II Corinthians 8:1,2 (Aramaic translation):
But we make known to you, my brothers, the grace of God that was given in the churches of the Macedonians,
that in the great trial of their pressure, [there] was an abundance to their joy, and the depth of their poverty was surpassed by the wealth of their open-handed giving.

The Macedonians are used as an example of the process of the grace of giving. The grace of God was poured out in the midst of great pressure and tribulation. They had been in the middle of despair caused by deep poverty. But this poverty was banished by the "wealth of their open-handed giving." The word for liberality in the King James and "open-handed giving" in this translation is often translated simplicity. The Aramaic root verb for simplicity means to "stretch out the hand with openness." In our culture we would say that a person was very generous. (Remember the simple life?) This generosity had banished the depth of their poverty and brought abundance to their lives. The passage then goes on to explain 5 main steps of a cycle that happened in their lives so that this abundance of joy was realized. These are the 5 steps:

1) **They gave themselves to the Lord**
2) **They had a willingness to give**
3) **They performed the giving for the ministering of the saints**
4) **The grace of God was poured out**

85

THE GRACE OF GIVING

5) Result: thanksgiving to God

This process then started over again as a cycle to cause them to give their hearts to the Lord even <u>more</u> and to be <u>more</u> willing to give and to give <u>more</u>. <u>More</u> grace is poured out and <u>more</u> thanksgiving is the result. Let us look at the key verses in these chapters that explain these steps.

> **II Corinthians 8:3-5 (KJV):**
> **For to *their* power, I bear record, yea, and beyond *their* power, *they were* willing of themselves;**
> **Praying us with much intreaty that we would receive the gift, and *take upon us* the fellowship of the ministering to the saints.**
> **And *this they did*, not as we hoped, but first gave their own selves to the Lord, and unto us by the will of God.**

First they "gave their own selves" to the Lord. This is the primary step. Without beginning with worship and praise to God and the Lord Jesus Christ, any kind of giving is empty and unprofitable. I have heard people say that they tithed, but never got any results. The reason they tithed was not out of love for the Lord, but of necessity or some other motivation. When your heart is full of praise for all God has done for you, you want to give your whole life to Him. Remember the lesson of Abel?

This kind of giving of our lives to the Lord issues in a willingness to give financially. Paul said of the Achaeans (from the area of Corinth) that they had a "readiness to will" a year before (verse 11). The readiness is explained in II Corinthians 9:1, 2. The Achaeans had been willing to give financially to the ministering of the saints for over a year. This second step is summarized in II Corinthians 8:12: **"For if there be first a willing mind, *it is* accepted according to that a man hath, *and* not according to that he hath not."** It does not matter how much the amount of the giving is. Someone who is wealthy can give much more than someone else who does not have a great income. What does matter is the willingness.

The third step in the cycle is to actually perform the giving. All the statements about wanting to give are meaningless without following through with the performance.

II Corinthians 8:11 (KJV):
Now therefore perform the doing *of it*; that as *there* was a readiness to will, so *there may be* a performance also out of that which ye have.

This giving does not yield an inequality, where one person is eased and another burdened. But there is a supply for the service of the saints, so that everyone's needs are met and there is no one who lacks. In chapter 9, the key verse for this step is verse 6: **"But this *I say*, He which soweth sparingly shall reap also sparingly; and he which soweth bountifully shall reap also bountifully."** This bountiful giving yields an increase. Because of the cheerful giving, God is able to pour out His grace so that there is sufficiency for every good work.

II Corinthians 9:8 9 (KJV):
And God *is* able to make all grace abound toward you; that ye always having all sufficiency in all *things*, may abound to every good work,

That is why this process is called "grace." Grace is given back to the giver all out of proportion to the amount given. The emphasis in verse 8 on all grace abounds, always having sufficiency in all things, unto every good work shows how God is abundant in His blessings being poured back to the one who gives. In fact, He is the one, who gives the "seed" to the one giving initially, and also provides his daily bread, multiplies the amount given and increases the fruit of his righteousness.

THE GRACE OF GIVING

How great and loving our God is to provide in such an abundant fashion!

When this abundance has been realized, it causes great thanksgiving back to God.

II Corinthians 9:11, 12 (KJV):
Being enriched in every thing to all bountifulness, which causeth through us thanksgiving to God.
For the administration of this service not only supplieth the want of the saints, but is abundant also by many thanksgivings unto God;

ENRICHED IN EVERYTHING! One cannot help but pour out his heart with rejoicing and thanksgiving for the sufficiency abounding in his life. This issues then in a continuation of the cycle. Because of seeing all that God had done for us, we want to give ourselves <u>more</u> to Him. We become <u>more</u> willing to give, and next time, to sow <u>more</u> bountifully because we understand the process. When you see the thankfulness welling up in your life, then you know that you are practicing the grace of giving. This is a cycle. You cannot have the end result of thanksgiving without the other steps.

To summarize, let's review the first questions we posed. It is clear that there is a process to giving which is a cycle. If someone is not getting results from their giving, examine the process to see if any of the steps in the cycle are missing. The whole cycle is a flow and can be started or stopped at anytime. What do we give and how? We first need to give of ourselves to the Lord in praise and honor to Him for all He has done for us. Then we give of our financial resources (out of what we have). We sow as bountifully as possible, so the increase will be bountiful also. We do the giving with a cheerful heart. We should follow up on our promises and spoken pledges to give for specific needs of the service of the saints, and perform "the doing of it." Then God is ABLE to make all grace abound and cause us to be **"enriched in everything,"** which results in great thanksgiving to God! This grace of giving is available to anyone who applies these principles and it is my prayer that this grace will abound in <u>your</u> life unto every good work.

Study Questions

1) Evaluate the giving that you are currently practicing and check your practice against the steps in the cycle. Are there any holes? Or do you see why you have been "enriched in everything?"
2) How does the often-quoted phrase **"God loveth a cheerful giver"** fit into this cycle?
3) In what categories of your life do you desire to be enriched? Make a list of specific areas where you would like to see <u>more</u> grace abounding.
4) What happens when you, like the Macedonians, give out of your need? Can you think of specific incidents in your life to document when you can honestly say that there was a **"wealth of open handed giving?"**

Chapter 13
Fruit in Your Account

The lessons in this book have covered almost all of the commonly taught Scriptures on giving. This last chapter touches on the subject of giving as it relates to "fruit." There are quite a number of Christians who teach that when you give to an organization, you are planting a seed and you will reap the harvest. You can choose some of the books in the bibliography if you wish to study this teaching further. John Avanzini and Kenneth Copeland are two teachers who use this metaphor extensively. They particularly use the verse in II Corinthians 9:6, **"He which soweth sparingly shall reap also sparingly; and he which soweth bountifully shall reap also bountifully."** Although the picture of giving as sowing is valid, I prefer to look at this section in Philippians as a picture of accounting, so that the imagery becomes clear. Let's first read the passage in Philippians.

> **Philippians 4:10-13 (Aramaic Translation):**
> **Now I rejoice greatly in our Lord that you have begun [again] to care for me, even as you were caring, but you were not able.**
> **Now I do not say [this] because I am in want, for I have learned that what I have will be enough for me.**
> **I know [how] to be humble. I know also [how] to abound in every [situation], and I am disciplined in all things, whether in fullness or in famine, in abundance or in want.**
> **I find strength for everything in Christ who strengthens me.**

ENRICHED IN EVERYTHING

The Philippians as a group had given gifts to Paul on several occasions during his travels in Macedonia and Achaia. Now that he is in prison in Rome, they have renewed their concern for him and have sent him a gift. This first portion of the passage emphasizes that Paul was very grateful, not so much for what the gift did for him as for the willingness of the Philippians to share with him. It was not relief of this need that primarily concerned him. He had learned to be content with what God provided. He was grateful because the Philippians had accepted his troubles as their own and had done something about it. The common translation of verse 13, "I can do all things" is beautifully portrayed in Aramaic as, **"I find strength for everything in Christ who strengthens me."** No matter whether there is plenty or want, Christ is our sufficiency. The strength to go on is FOUND, not because of any ability of our own. Paul did not seek the gift, yet because it was given, there was tremendous thanksgiving. This sounds like the grace of giving, doesn't it?

This passage has a number of terms that relate to accounting and business. I am a bookkeeper by profession, so the descriptions come readily to mind as I handle paying bills and keeping track of receipts for my clients. I have made a chart to draw out the comparison which will clarify the usage of the different terms.

VERSE	WORD USED	DEFINITION	FINANCIAL MEANING
11, 12	In want	Lack, in want or need, have loss	No funds in the bank
15, 19	Need	Need, necessity (in any category)	Bills to pay (e.g., credit cards)
16	Necessity	Ordinary necessities of life	Purchases needed to make

11	Enough	Sufficient, enough	Bank balance equal to all the bills
14, 15	Contributed, Communicated	Contribute, participate with	Write checks, distribute payments
15	Receiving and giving	Receive in terms of acceptance	Deposits and withdrawals
17	Fruit	Any kind of profit, benefits	Net profit
17	Account	Be multiplied	Interest
18	Received	Received full payment	Payment with receipt
18	Have abundance	Abound, have plenty	Balance left in bank

Now have fun finding all the uses of the words on this chart in the whole passage.

Philippians 4:14-19 (Aramaic translation):
Nevertheless, you have done well to have contributed for my difficulties.
Now you know also, Philippians, that in the beginning of the gospel when I left Macedonia, not even one of the churches communicated with me with regard [to] receiving and giving, but you only,
so that even at Thessalonica once and again you sent to me my need.
[It is] not that I seek a gift, but I desire that fruit should multiply to you.
I have received everything and I have abundance and I am full. And I have accepted all that you have sent to me by way of Epaphroditus, a sweet

**fragrance, and a welcomed sacrifice that is pleasing to God.
And my God will supply all your need according to his riches in the glory of Jesus Christ.**

There are three words used for need: necessity, need and want or lack. The difference between the three is seen in the financial illustration above. To be in want means that to have no money in the bank, or at least not enough. To have need means that we have accounts payable, bills to pay. (I used credit cards as an example, because they are the bills that most often "sneak up" on us and end up being larger than the balance in the bank.) Necessities are the things that we need to buy for the ordinary daily living: food, clothes, and housing. The word comes from the verb, to use, so a necessity is something we use often. When we are in want, we need some deposits to increase the bank account. When we are in need, we need to pay the bills. When we have necessity, we need to make purchases for daily living.

When the Philippians gave to Paul, he called it "communicating with me." To communicate means to participate or share in some fashion. If we share in meeting a need, then it is like we are writing the checks for the bills. There is a distribution of the cash in the bank for the bills. There is a partnership or fellowship relationship in this sense. That is also why Paul described the communication as receiving and giving, for these are the deposits and withdrawals from the bank balance. When a check is deposited at the bank, it is accepted and you receive a receipt for the amount. THEN you can write checks. So we need to receive first, then give. And it is a two-way transaction.

Other verses that use the word "communicate" are worthy to note here. Romans 12:13 says, **"Communicate to the need of the saints."** In Romans 15:26 it states, **"those who were in Macedonia and Achaia desired to participate in sharing with the poor saints that are in Jerusalem."**

Galatians 6:6 adds that **"he who has heard the word should communicate to that [one] who instructed him, in all good things."** This kind of communicating pleases God as in Hebrews 13:16, **"And do not forget compassion and sharing with the poor, for with these sacrifices a man pleases God."**

In verse 18, Paul says, **"I have received everything."** In Greek, this is the word *apecho* and is the technical term for drawing up a receipt. It is used in the papyri regarding business transactions. The RSV translated this phrase, **I have received full payment."** The amount given by the Philippians was "sufficient," in other words, after the gift was deposited, the bank balance had enough to cover all the bills. To have enough means to be equal to. Then Paul adds in verse 18, that not only was there enough, but **"I have abundance"** or more than enough, plenty in reserve. I paid off the lines of credit and still had a balance in the bank!

Another interesting usage of this passage is calling the gift of the Philippians **"a sweet fragrance and a welcomed sacrifice that is pleasing to God."** This reminds us of the meal offerings in the Old Testament that would smell so sweet with the burning of the frankincense on the altar. The sweet smell had to do with God's acceptance of the offering. And the point of calling it a sacrifice is that ANY kind of offering is a sacrifice. It is accepted according to what a man has, not what he does not have. In the Old Testament, if you were poor, two turtledoves was a proper sacrifice. If you were wealthier, the appropriate sacrifice would be a bullock. Remember the widow who put in two mites to the temple box? Jesus said that she put in everything she had, all her goods (Mark 12:44). Now that was truly a sacrifice. Out of her need, she gave, but trusting that God would supply the want in her life. The amount of the gift is not the important part; it is the heart with which it is given.

Then the best point of all the passage has to do with fruit. Fruit is profit of any kind and is used in many different contexts. We could say benefits, or interest, in financial terminology. Paul did not want their gift only for what it would do to communicate with his need, but the best part is that it would allow interest to be accrued in THEIR account. Now the greatest part about giving is that it does not diminish the resources of the giver. He always gets interest multiplied back to him! The reason God does this is so that there can be a free flow back and forth between people. It is summed up in II Corinthians 8.

> **II Corinthians 8:13-15 (Aramaic translation):**
> **For it is not that others should have relief, and you pressure,**
> **But [that] you should be in balance. At this time, that your abundance might be to their need, that also their abundance be to your need, so that there be a balance.**
> **As it is written, He who received much did not have excess, and he who received little did not lack.**

At one time, you have an abundance to give to me. At another I have an abundance to give to you. Then there are different bills to pay, so there are different needs. It may be that one person has a financial need and another a spiritual need for healing or for instruction. The goal is that all the needs are met. And God is the one who is the supplier, because he works in the hearts of the believers to care for each other.

The word need in Philippians 4:19 is this word for any kind of bill. Your need may be for understanding, mine may be for help with my children, and Susie might need health. The list can go on and on. Do you agree now that "communicating" is a good word to describe this process of giving?

FRUIT IN YOUR ACCOUNT

Summary

Since this book has been a study that would allow personal reflection and/or discussion in a small group, please use this last lesson as a time for summarizing things learned. Either use it as a place to go back over the lessons and write down conclusions and practical application of the specific points, or use it in your group to review the chapters one by one and to look back on the things that you have discussed. Please review how these lessons will affect your lives in the future.

There are several Greek words to study in the New Testament. They are either translated giving or have to do with giving. These are presented here for your further work in this field. The verses listed are only representative uses of the words..

1)	*logia*	Collection	I Cor. 16:1, 2
2)	*charis*	Grace	I Cor 16:1, 3, II Cor 8:4
3)	*koinonia*	Fellowship	II Cor 8:4, 9:13
4)	*diakonia*	Service	II Cor 8:4, 9:1, 12,13
5)	*hadrotes*	Abundance	II Cor 8:20
6)	*eulogia*	Blessing	II Cor 9:5
7)	*leitourgia*	Ministration	II Cor 9:12
8)	*eleemosune*	Alms	Acts 24:17
9)	*prosphora*	Offerings	Acts 24:17

There are so many aspects of the topic of giving that we have explored. The beginning lessons showed how all giving is to be motivated by love and must be conformed to God's direction in obedience. We must look to the Most High God as the source and way of provision. We learned also that the first fruits are what redeem the rest of the increase of our fields, animals, and children. In the chapter on types of offerings, we were reminded that giving is to provide for God's ministers, as the Levites were to the children of Israel. Hezekiah was a great example of how to administer giving and the chapter on blessings confirmed God's promises to us as the result of our giving. We became aware of areas in which it is easy to cheat. We saw who really are the poor and how to give true charity. The simple life is lifestyle to emulate, in always being generous, not stingy. Luke enjoined us to forgive and not to judge, and reminded us that the measure of our giving will be measured to us again. We saw how God is the ultimate example of giving freely and how to apply the process of the grace of giving. Finally, in this chapter we looked at the accounting aspect of giving and receiving.

As we come to the close of the lessons in this book, I am full of some of the same desire that Paul must have had for the Philippians. I desire that fruit be multiplied to your account, that you have all the benefits and blessings you need and MORE THAN ENOUGH. I believe that studying the lessons in the whole Bible on giving has allowed us to ponder some of the application to our own lives – I know it has for me, and I truly pray that would be the case for you also. I would like to thank you for the opportunity to share some of this learning with you and for allowing me to be able to "communicate" with you regarding this wonderful topic. May God enrich you in everything according to his bountiful wealth in Christ Jesus as you continue to practice "open handed giving!"

Bibliography

Angus, Joseph and Green, Samuel G., ed. *The Bible Hand-Book: An Introduction to the Study of Sacred Scripture.* New York: Fleming H. Revell Co, 1902.

Avanzini, John. *30, 60, Hundredfold.* Tulsa, Oklahoma: Harrison House, 1989.

Barker, Kenneth, et al. *The NIV Study Bible.* Grand Rapids, Michigan: Zondervan Publishing House, 1995.

Barnes, Charles Randall, ed. *The People's Bible Encyclopedia.* Chicago: The People's Publication Society, 1921.

Bell, Albert A., Jr. *A Guide to the New Testament World.* Scottsdale, Pennsylvania: Herald Press, 1994.

Benton, Henry. *The Manners and Customs of the Jews and Other Nations Mentioned in the Bible.* Hartford Publishers, 1839.

Bivin, David and Roy Blizzard Jr. *Understanding the Difficult Words of Jesus.* Austin, Texas: Center for Judaic-Christian Studies, 1984.

Black, Matthew. *An Aramaic Approach to the Gospel & Acts.* London: Oxford at the Clarendon Press, 1946.

Bowen, Barbara M. *Strange Scriptures That Perplex the Western Mind.* Grand Rapids, Michigan: William B. Eerdmans Publishing, 1973.

Brown, Francis, S.R. Driver, Charles A. Briggs, eds. *The New Brown-Driver-Briggs-Gesenius Hebrew and English Lexicon.* Christian Copyrights, Inc., 1983.

Brown, Raymond E., Joseph A. Fitzmyer, Roland E. Murphy. *The Jerome Biblical Commentary.* Englewood Cliffs, New Jersey: Prentice-Hall, Inc., 1968.

Bullians, Andrew M. *Health, Wealth & Wisdom.* Lima, Ohio: Fairway Press, 1996.

Bullinger, E. W. *A Critical Lexicon and Concordance to the English and Greek New Testament.* Grand Rapids, Michigan: Zondervan Publishing House, 1975.

Bullinger, E. W. *Great Cloud of Witnesses.* Grand Rapids, Michigan: Kregel Publications, 1979.

Burder, Samuel. *Oriental Customs: Or An Illustration of the Sacred Scriptures.* 2 vols. London: Longman, Hurst, Rees, & Orme, 1808.

Daniel-Rops, Henri. *Daily Life in the Times of Jesus.* New York: Hawthorn Books, Inc., 1962.

Douglas, J. D, ed. *New Bible Dictionary.* Wheaton, Illinois: Tyndale House Publishers, 1987.

BIBLIOGRAPHY

Duckat, Walter. *Beggar to King: All the Occupations of Biblical Times.* New York: Doubleday & Company, 1969.

Edersheim, Alfred. *Sketches of Jewish Social Life.* Grand Rapids, Michigan: William B. Eerdmans Publishing, 1982.

Edersheim, Alfred. *The Life and Times of Jesus the Messiah.* McLean, Virginia: MacDonald Publishing Company, 1886 reprint.

Edersheim, Alfred. *The Temple.* Grand Rapids, Michigan: William B. Eerdmans Publishing, 1978.

Fairweather, William. *The Background of the Epistles.* Minneapolis: Klock & Klock Christian Publishers, 1977.

Freeman, James M. *Manners and Customs of the Bible.* Plainfield, New Jersey: Logos International, 1972.

Gaebelein, Frank E. *The Expositor's Bible Commentary.* Grand Rapids, Michigan: Zondervan Publishing House, 1984.

Girdlestone, Robert Baker. *Synonyms of the Old Testament.* Grand Rapids, Michigan: William B. Eerdmans Publishing, 1897 reprint.

Gower, Ralph. *New Manners and Customs of the Bible.* Chicago: Moody Press, 1987.

Habershon, Ada R. *Study of the Types.* Grand Rapids, Michigan: Kregel Publications, 1974.

Harris, R. Laird, Gleason L. Archer, Jr., Bruce K. Waltke, eds. *Theological Wordbook of the Old Testament. 2 vols.* Chicago: Moody Press, 1980.

Hartman, Louis F., ed. *Encyclopedic Dictionary of the Bible.* New York: McGraw-Hill Book Co., 1963.

Jacobus, Melancthon W. and Elbert C. Lane, Andrew C. Zenos, ed. *Funk & Wagnall's New Standard Bible Dictionary.* Garden City, New York: Garden City Books, 1936.

Jennings, William. *Lexicon to the Syriac New Testament.* London: Oxford University Press, 1926.

Jukes, Andrew. *The Law of the Offerings.* Grand Rapids, Michigan: Kregel Publications, 1997.

Jukes, Andrew. *Types in Genesis.* Grand Rapids, Michigan: Kregel Publications, 1976.

Kaiser, Walter. *The Messiah in the Old Testament.* Grand Rapids, Michigan: Zondervan Publishing House, 1995.

BIBLIOGRAPHY

Lamsa, George M. *Gospel Light, A Revised Annotated Edition.* Aramaic Bible Society, 1999.

Lamsa, George M. *Idioms in the Bible Explained and a Key to the Original Gospels.* San Francisco: Harper & Row, Publishers, 1985.

Lamsa, George M. *The Modern New Testament.* Marina Del Rey, California: De Vorss Publications, 1998.

Lewis, Agnes Smith. *A Translation of the Four Gospels from the Syriac of the Sinaitic Palimsest.* London: MacMillan and Co., 1894.

Lewis, Agnes Smith. *Light on the Four Gospels from the Siniatic Palimpsest.* London: Williams & Norgate, 1912.

Lightfoot, John. *A Commentary on the New Testament from the Talmud and Hebraica. 4 vols.* Peabody, Massachusetts: Hendrickson Publishers, 1989.

Mackie, George M. *Bible Manners and Customs.* New York: Fleming H. Revell Co., 1898.

Matthews, Victor H. *Manners and Customs in the Bible.* Peabody, Mass.: Hendrickson Publishers, 1988.

Miller, Madeleine S. *Encyclopedia of Bible Life.* New York: Harper & Brothers Publishing, 1944.

Moffatt, James. *A New Translation of the Bible.* New York: Harper & Row, Publishers, 1954.

Murdock, James, trans. *The New Testament.* New York: Stanford and Swords, 1852.

Nave, Orville J. *The New Nave's Topical Bible.* Grand Rapids, Michigan: Zondervan Publishing House, 1969.

Neil, James. *Everyday Life in the Holy Land.* London: Church Missions to Jews, 1953.

Neil, James. *Palestine Explored.* London: James Nisbet & Co., 1881.

Neil, James. *Peeps Into Palestine.* London: Henry J. Walter, 1944.

Packer, J.C. and Merrill C. Tenney. *Illustrated Manners and Customs of the Bible.* Nashville: Thomas Nelson Publishers, 1980.

Packer, J.C. and Merrill C. Tenney and William White Jr. *The Bible Almanac.* Carmel, New York: Guideposts, 1980.

Pentecost, J. Dwight. *The Parables of Jesus.* Grand Rapids, Michigan: Zondervan Publishing House, 1982.

BIBLIOGRAPHY

Rice, Edwin W. *Commentary on the Gospel According to Luke.* Philadelphia: The Union Press, 1914.

Rice, Edwin W. *Orientalisms in Bible Lands.* Philadelphia: American Sunday-School Union, 1910.

Rice, Edwin W. *People's Dictionary of the Bible.* Philadelphia: American Sunday-School Union, 1904.

Rihbany, Abraham Mitrie. *The Syrian Christ.* Boston: Houghton Mifflin Company, 1916.

Ritchie, John. *Feasts of Jehovah.* Grand Rapids, Michigan: Kregel Publications, 1982.

Ritchie, John. *Tabernacle in the Wilderness.* Grand Rapids, Michigan: Kregel Publications, 1982.

Smith, J. Payne. *A Compendious Syriac Dictionary.* London: Oxford at the Clarendon Press, 1967.

Tabor, James, ed. *Original Bible Project: Preliminary Edition, the Book of Genesis.* 1998.

Thayer, Joseph Henry. *The New Thayer's Greek-English Lexicon of the New Testament.* Christian Copyrights, Inc., 1981.

Trimm, James Scott. *The Rules of Hillel.* Austin, Texas: Society of Nazarene Judaism, 1999.

Trimm, James Scott. *The Semitic Origin of the New Testament.* Hurst, Texas: Hebrew/Aramaic New Testament Research, 1996.

Tucker, T. J. *Life in the Roman World of Nero and St. Paul.* New York: The Macmillan Company, 1929.

Van Deursen, A. *Illustrated Dictionary of Bible Manners and Customs.* New York: Philosophical Library Inc., 1967.

Van-Lennep, Henry J. *Bible Lands: Their Modern Customs and Manners.* New York: Harper & Brothers, 1875.

Weiss, G. Christian. *Insights Into Bible Times and Customs.* Chicago: Moody Press, 1974.

Wight, Fred H. *Manners and Customs of Bible Lands.* Chicago: Moody Press, 1953.

About the Author

Janet Magiera, with her husband Glen, are the founders of Light of the Word Ministry, a non-profit corporation under the E.M.A., the Evangelistic Messenger's Association. In 1978, under the inspiration of Dr. George M. Lamsa's work on the translation of the Bible from the Aramaic texts, Jan began pursuing a course of study of the Peshitta New Testament. For over 20 years, she has taught Bible studies, and worked with believers in Michigan, Ohio, Kansas, Tennessee, and California, using the insight from her work with the language.

The main goal of Light of the Word Ministry is to continue to make available the understanding of the Scriptures from Biblical customs, figures of speech, and the study of Aramaic. One of the projects currently in progress is a modern English translation of the Aramaic New Testament using a computer database. This will lead to the publication of an Aramaic lexicon, concordance, and analytical dictionary. The database uses a numbering system similar to Strong's that will enable laymen as well as scholars to study the language. Jan is currently writing two other volumes for *The Searchlight Series*. Another publication planned is a CD ROM of out-of-print books on Biblical customs.

The Aramaic Bible Society recently published a revised annotated edition of *Gospel Light* by Dr. George M. Lamsa, edited by Janet Magiera. It includes the insertion of the Estrangelo Aramaic script for all of the Aramaic words that are explained in the articles. Lamsa's books, often chastened by the critics, lacked the support for scholars in references and footnotes. Jan has supplied this lack by the addition of the confirming footnotes of scholars in Biblical literature, theology, and archaeological research.

Glen and Jan currently co-pastor a church in Irvine, California, and fellowship with other ministries around the nation.